DISCOVERING TOULOUSE FRANCE

The Pink City Pictorial

PICTORIAL SEARIES

Presented by

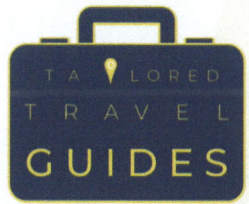

Discover your journey!

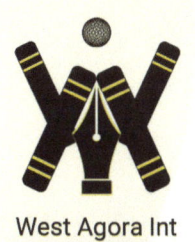

West Agora Int

a WEST AGORA INT S.R.L. Brand
www.tailoredtravelguides.com
Edited by WEST AGORA INT S.R.L.
WEST AGORA INT S.R.L. All Rights Reserved
Copyright © WEST AGORA INT S.R.L., 2023

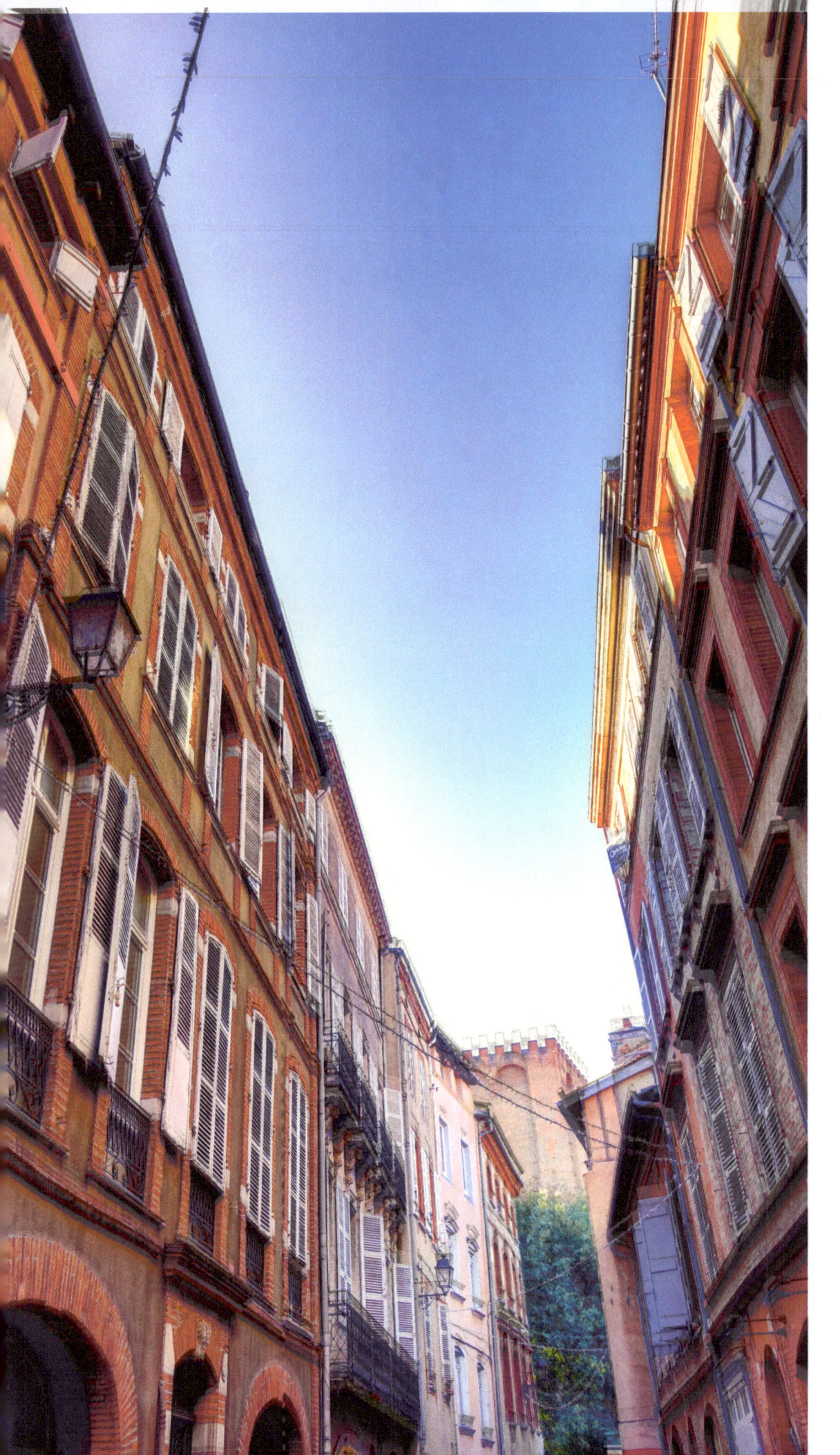

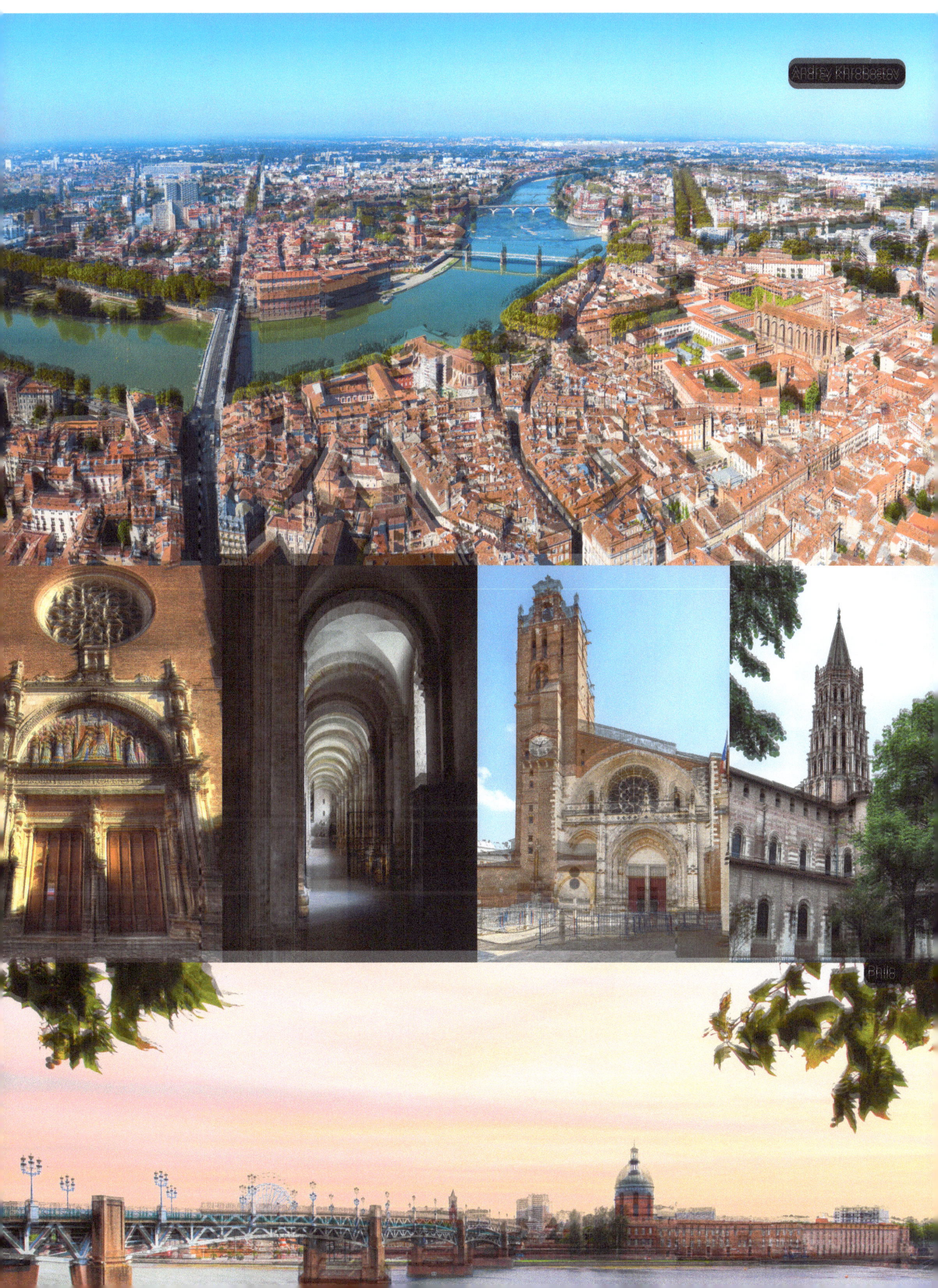

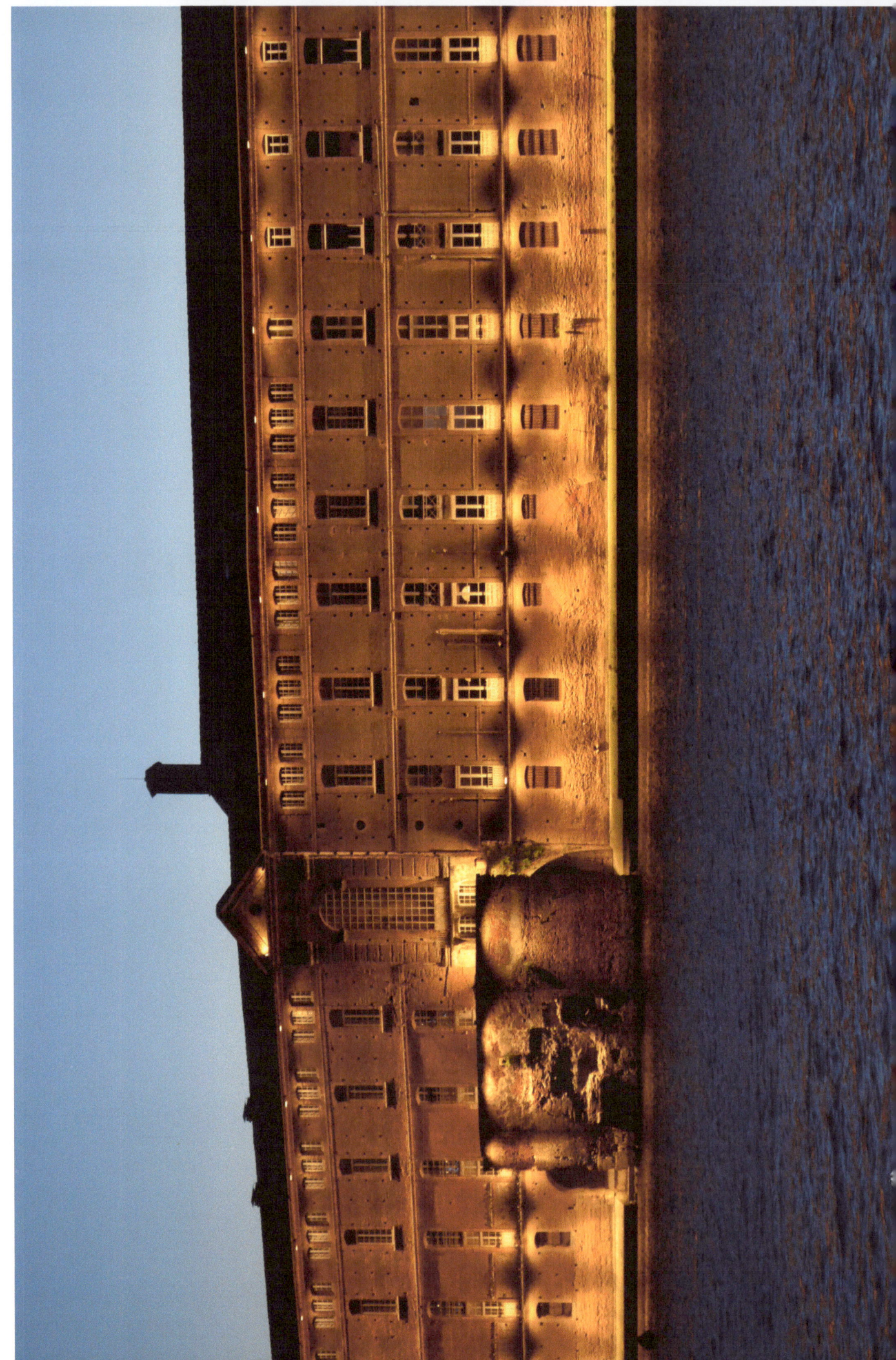

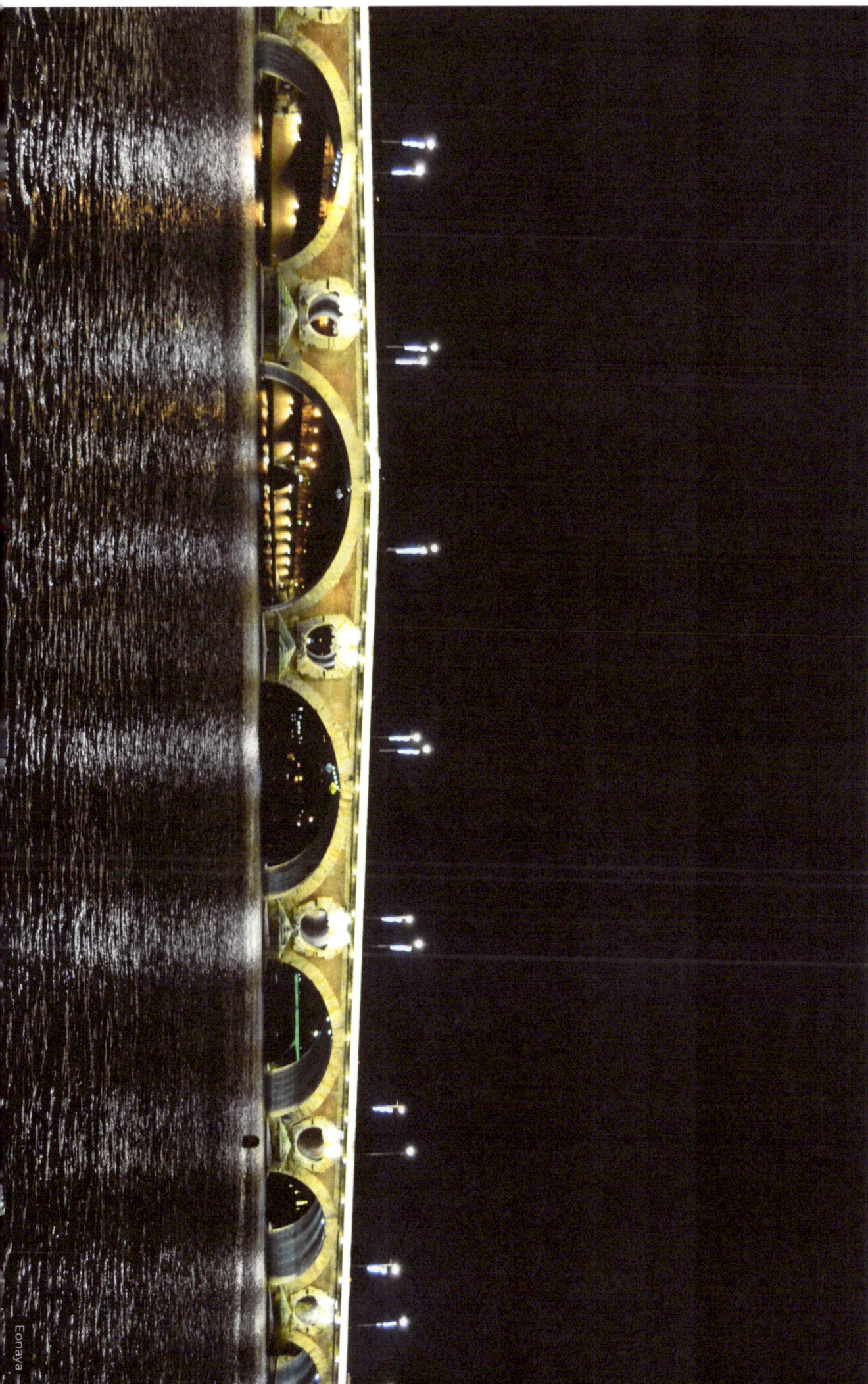

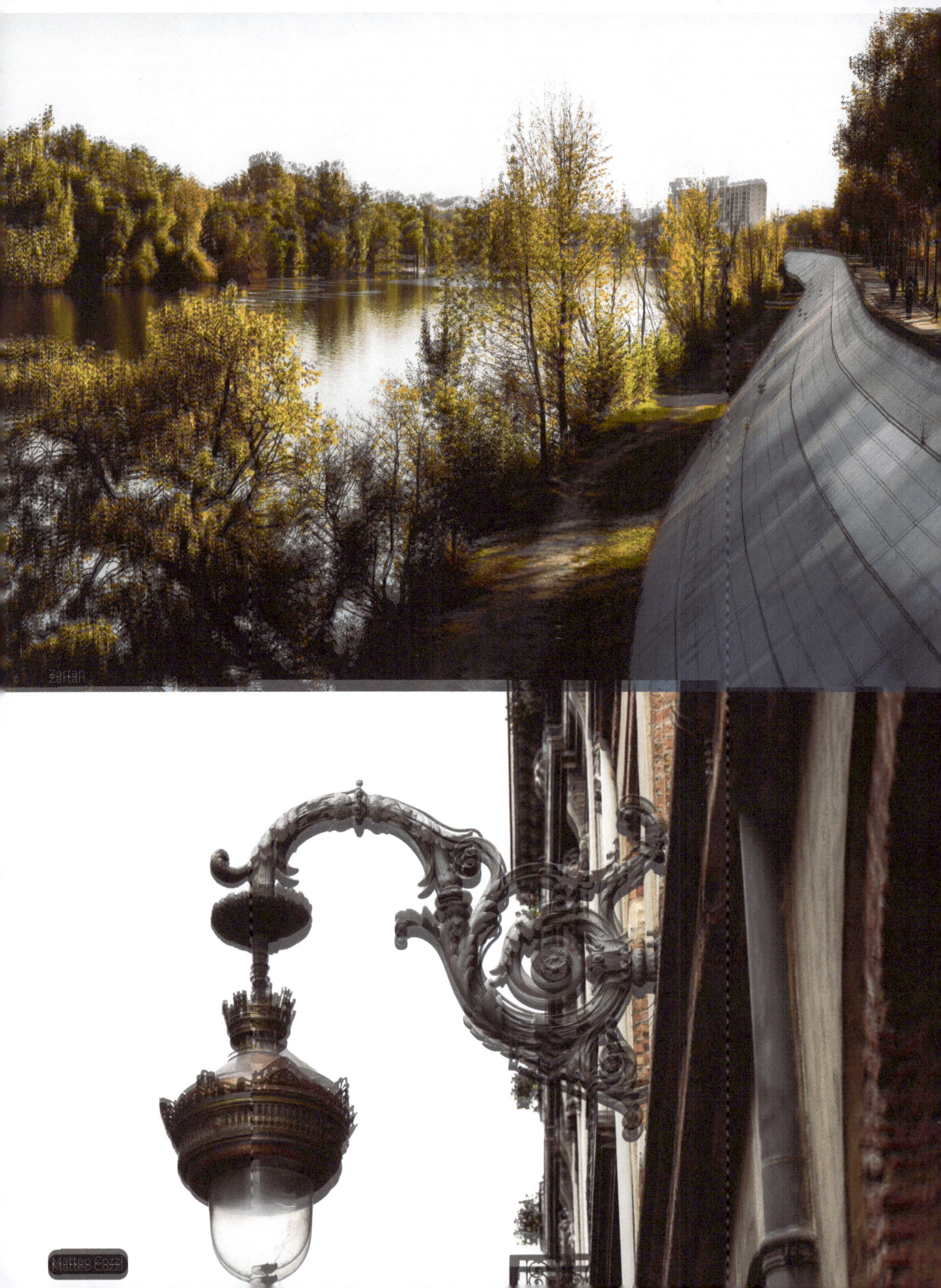

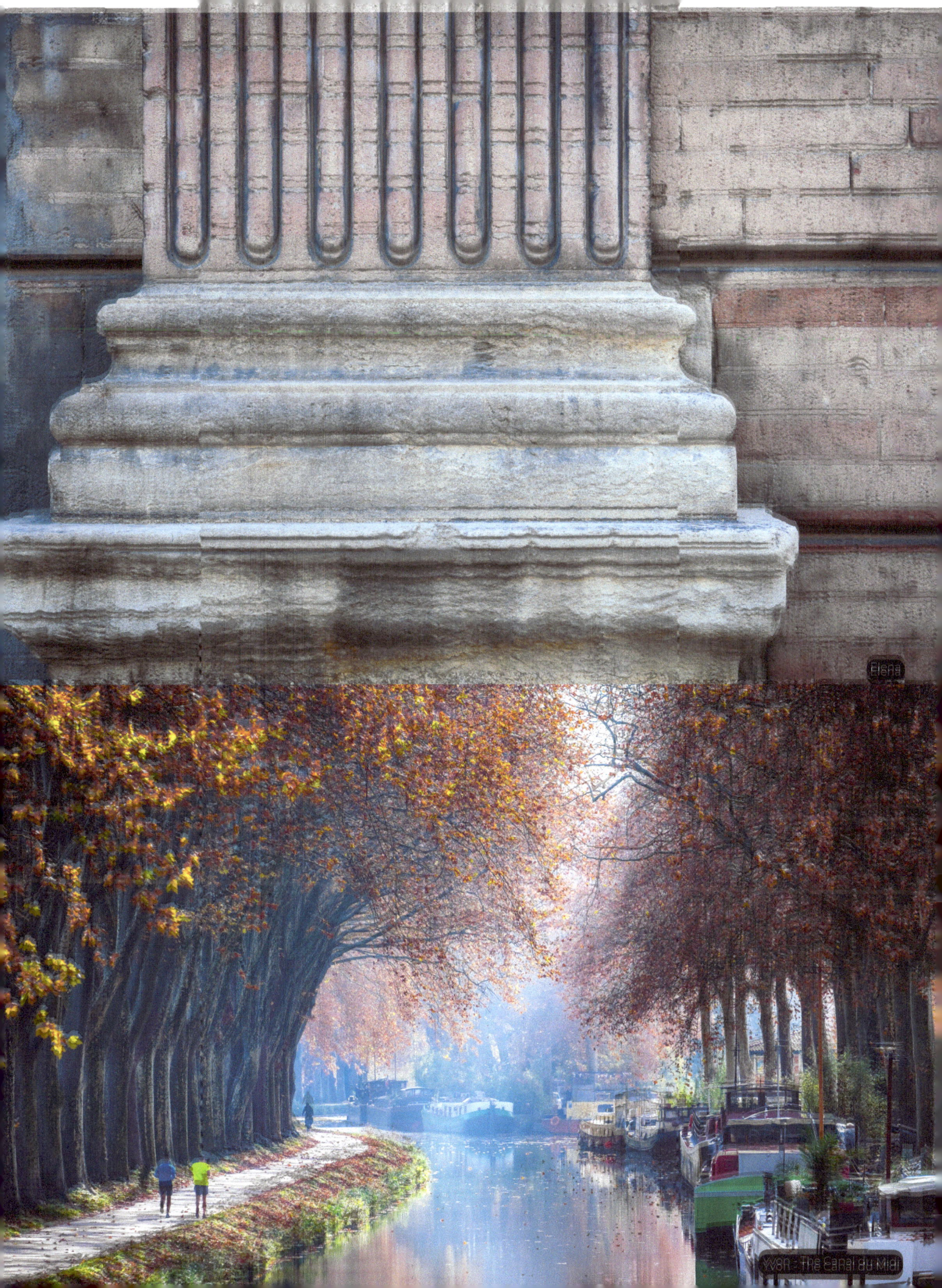

Cúpula de La Grave

Nestled along the banks of the Garonne River, the Cúpula de La Grave stands as an emblematic silhouette in Toulouse's skyline. This majestic dome, crowning the Hôpital de La Grave, presents a striking contrast against the city's predominantly pink architecture, a result of the terra cotta bricks prevalent in the region. The dome, completed in the early 20th century, showcases the grandeur of neoclassical design, with its façade gleaming in the southern French sun.

The Cúpula's interior is equally awe-inspiring. Its expansive space, adorned with intricate frescoes and gilded accents, exudes an air of solemnity and grace. Historically a sanctuary for the sick, it now serves as a poignant reminder of Toulouse's enduring commitment to compassion and healthcare.

The dome's vantage point offers panoramic views of La Ville Rose, providing a unique perspective of the city's harmonious blend of historic and contemporary urban landscapes. The Garonne, with its tranquil flow, complements the dome's serene presence, creating picturesque scenes that captivate photographers and artists alike.

Visiting the Cúpula de La Grave is more than a visual delight; it's an immersive journey into the heart of Toulouse's rich heritage, where architectural beauty and historical depth converge.

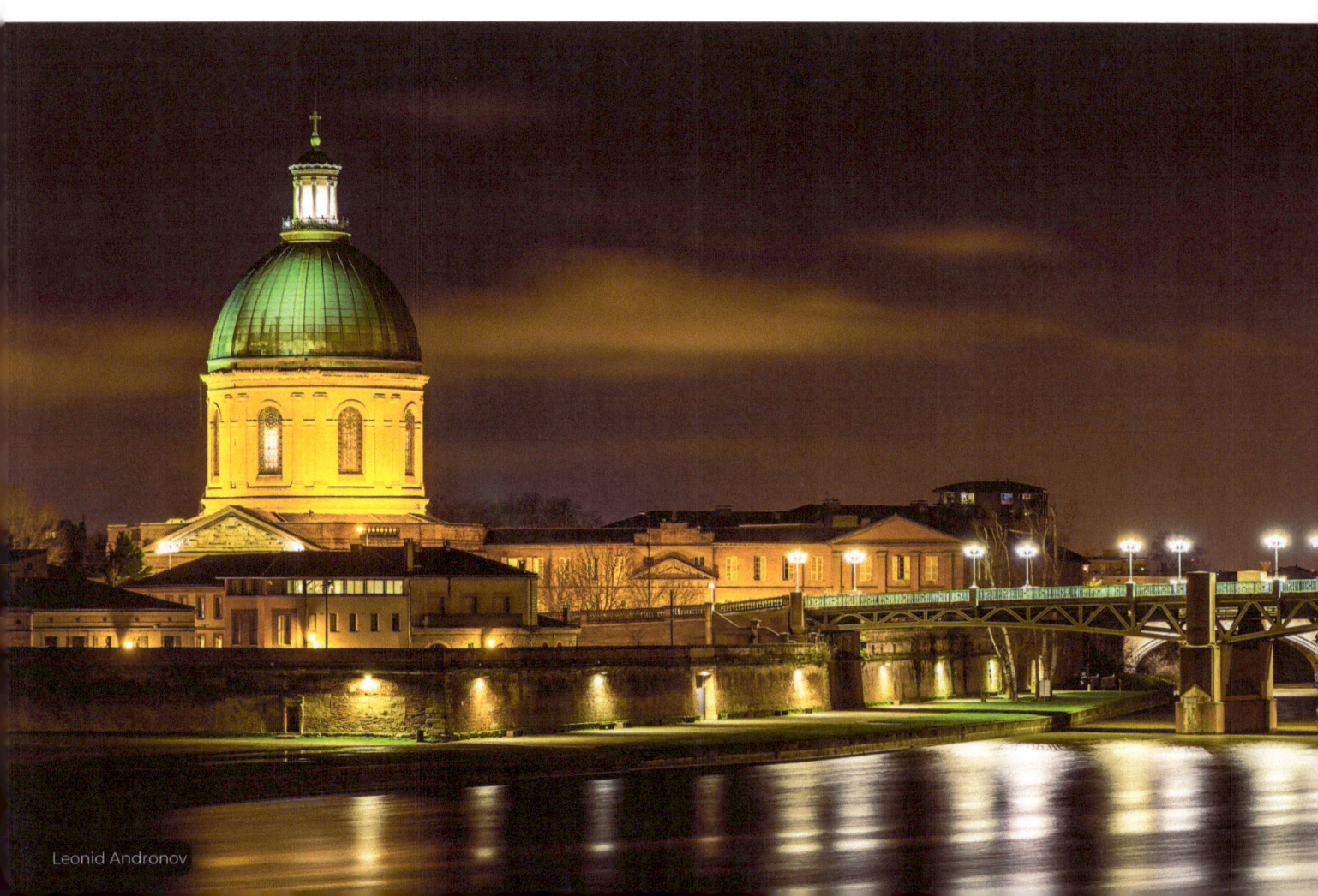

Leonid Andronov

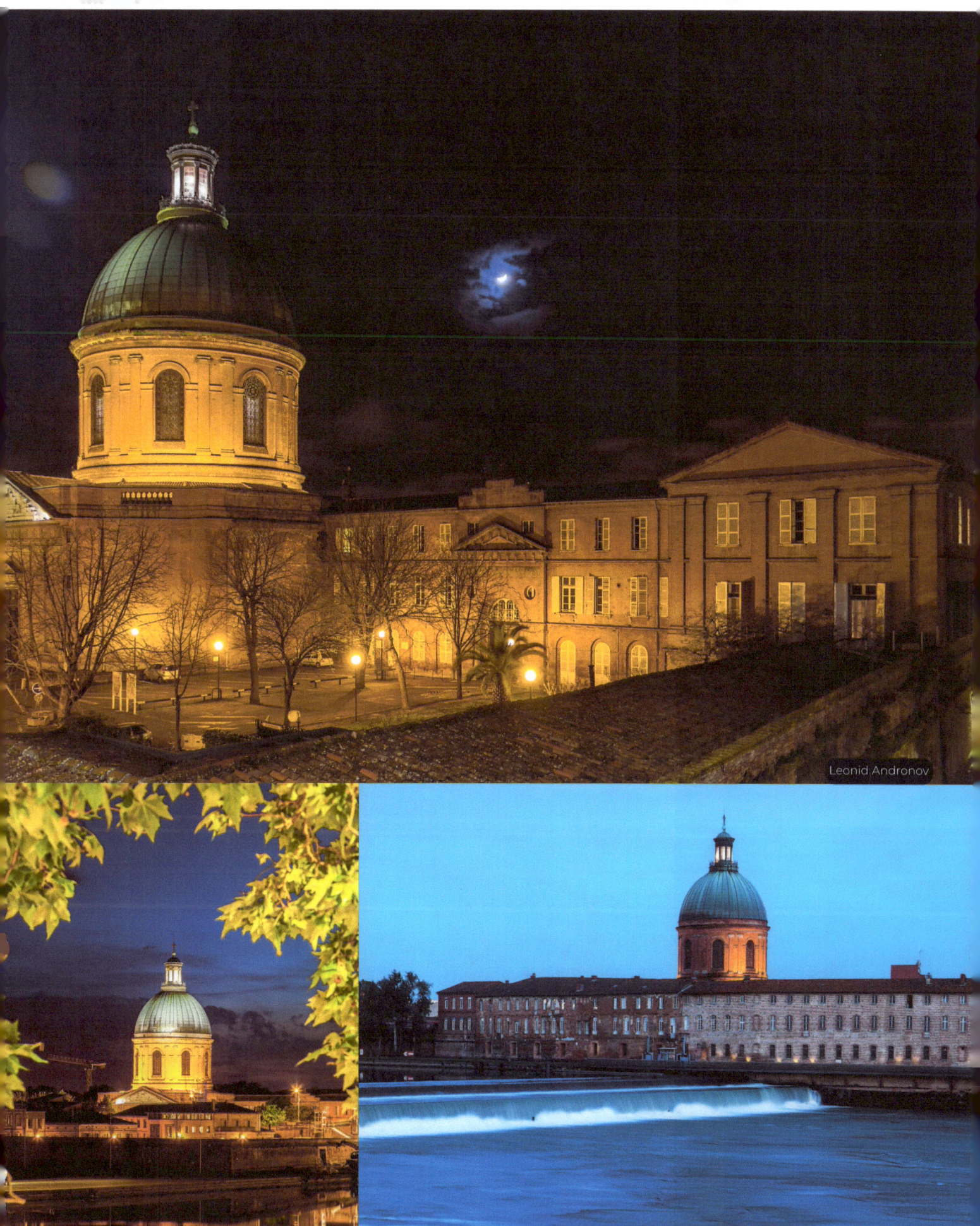

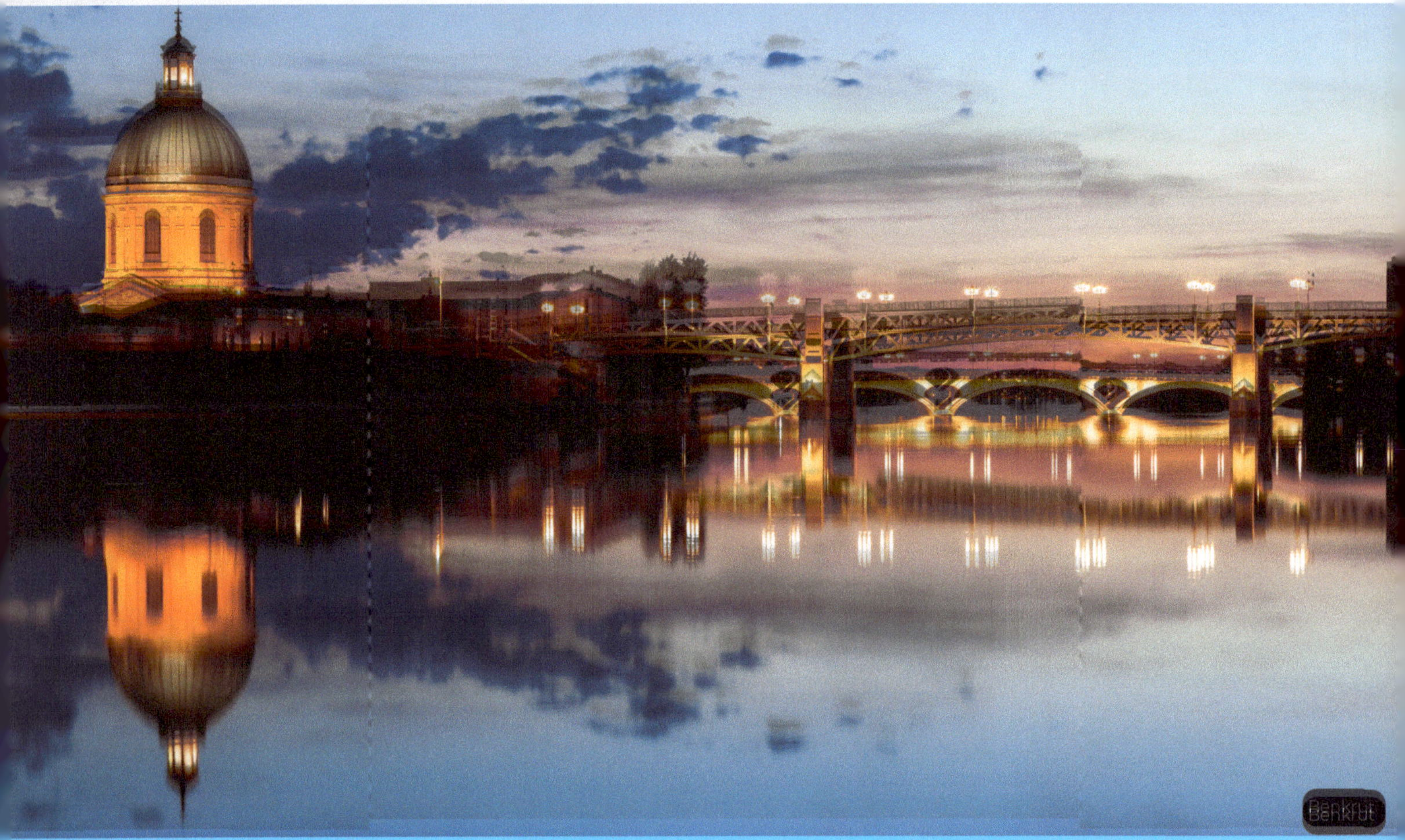

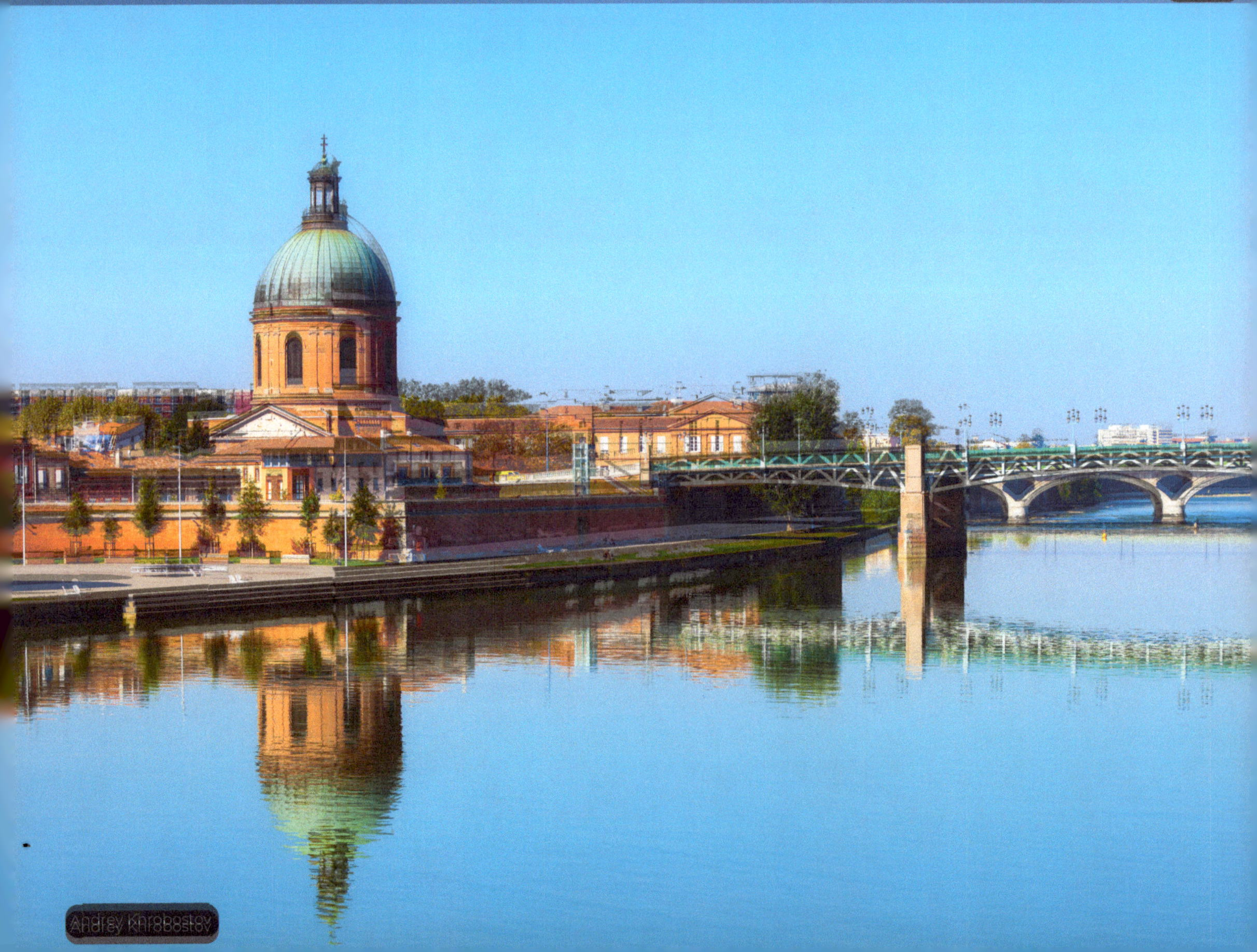

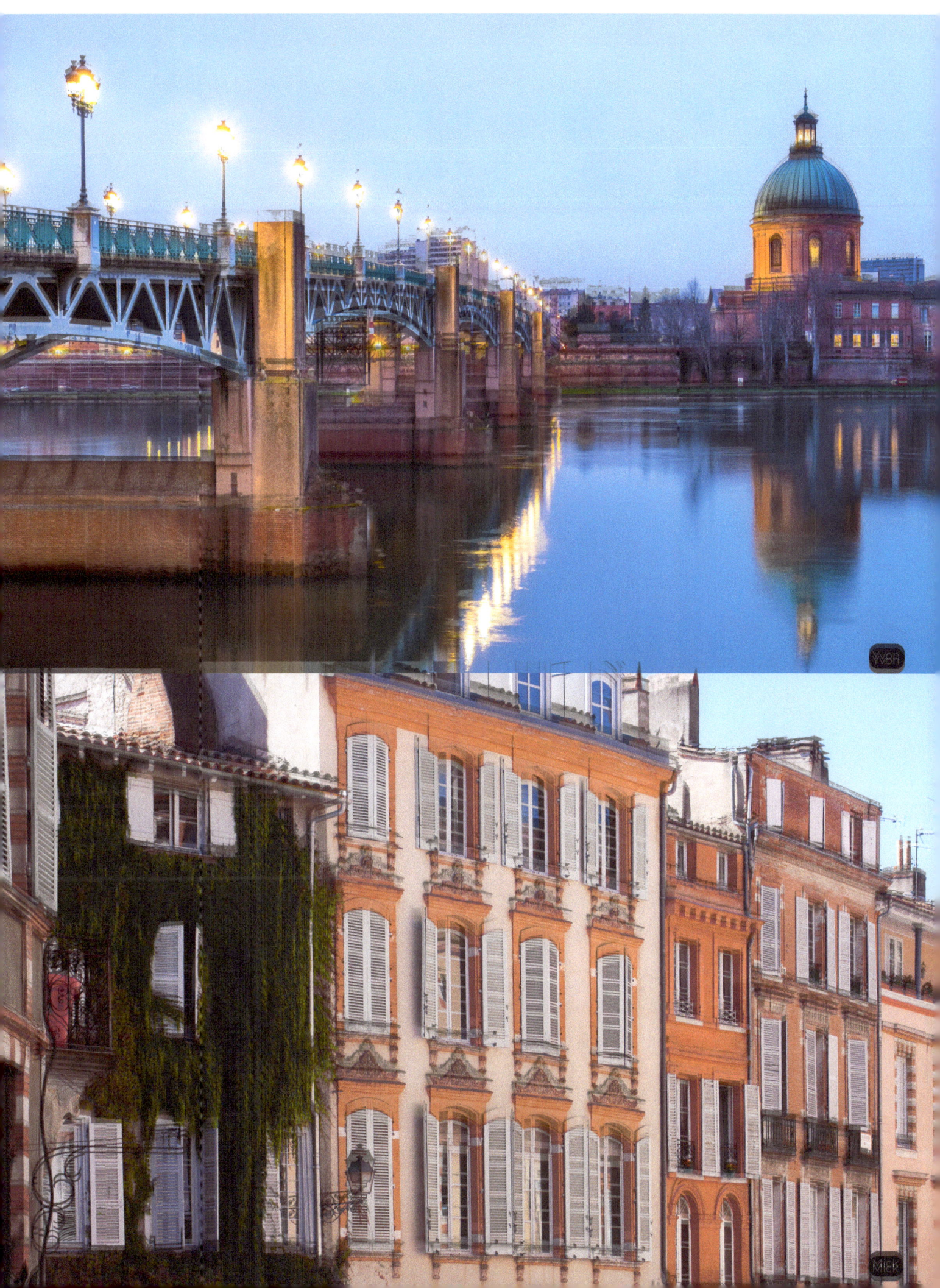

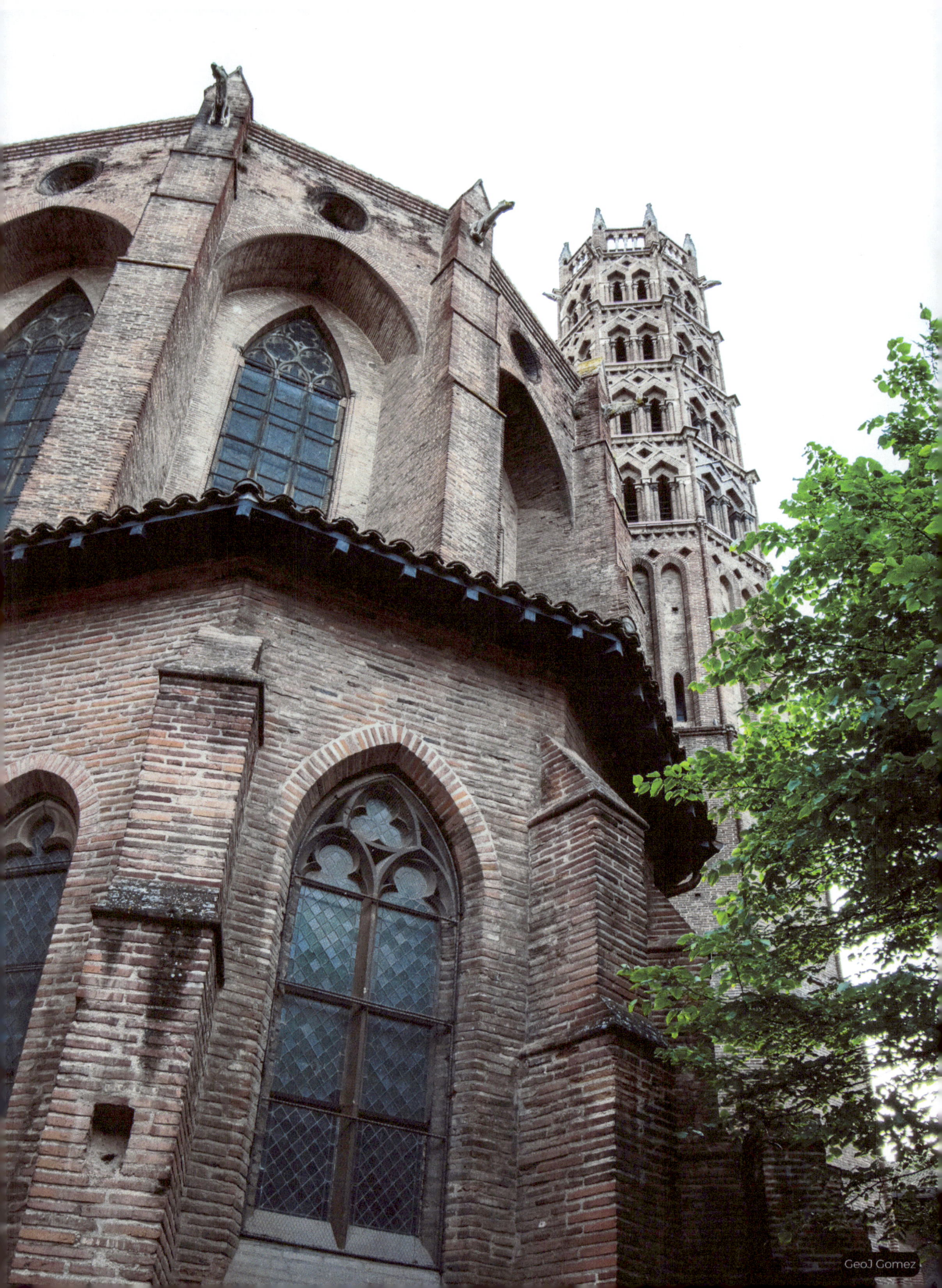

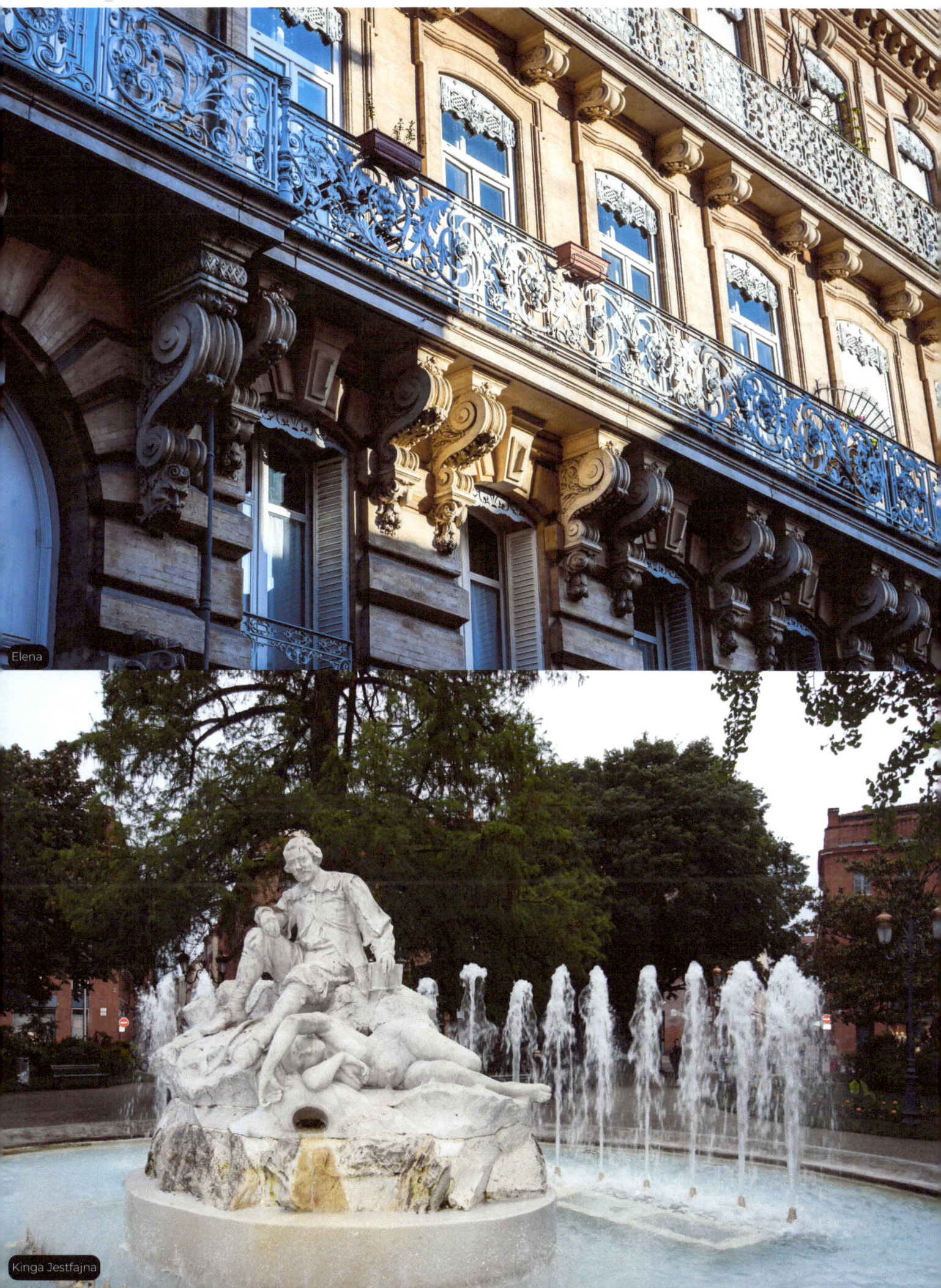

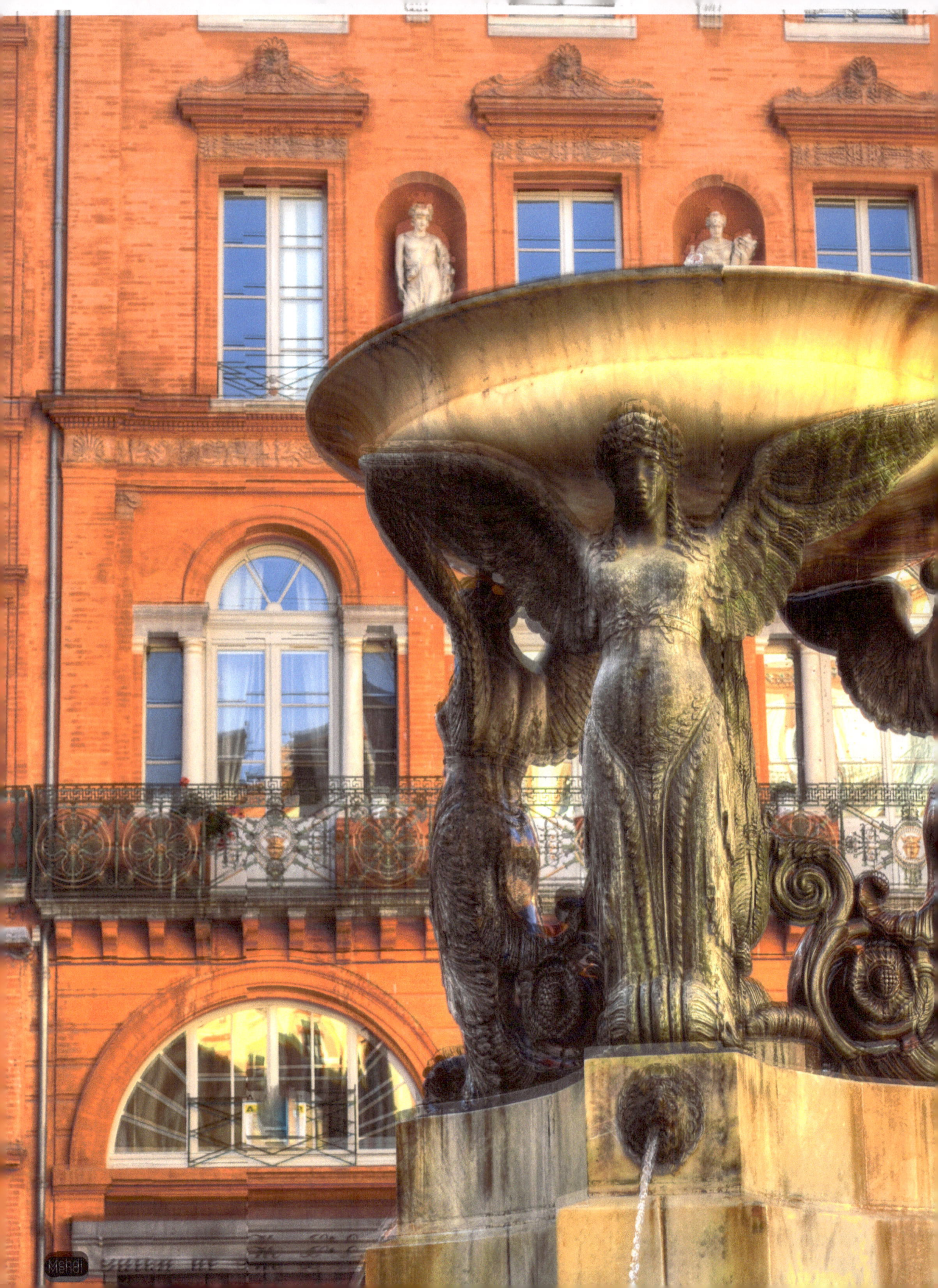

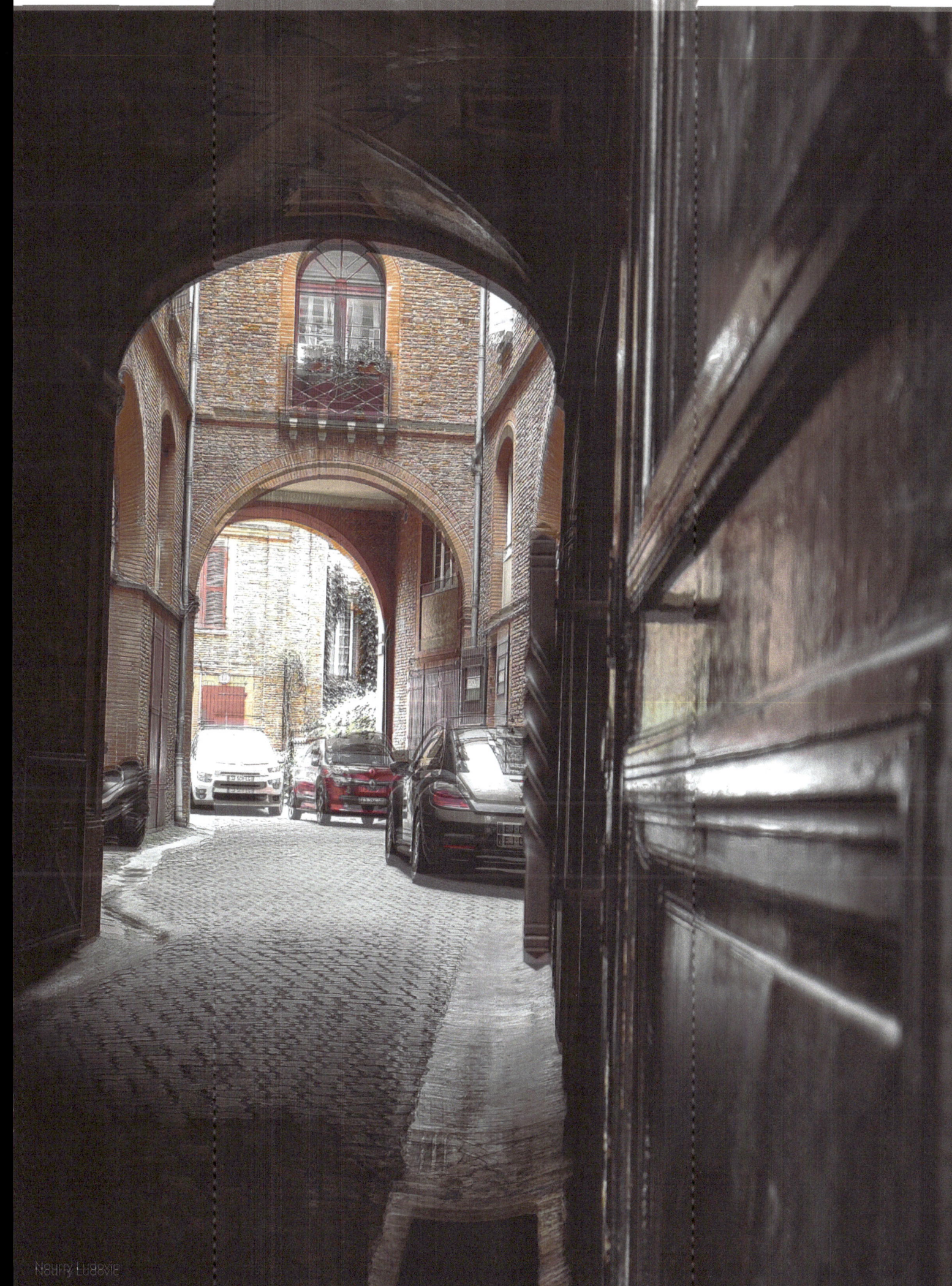

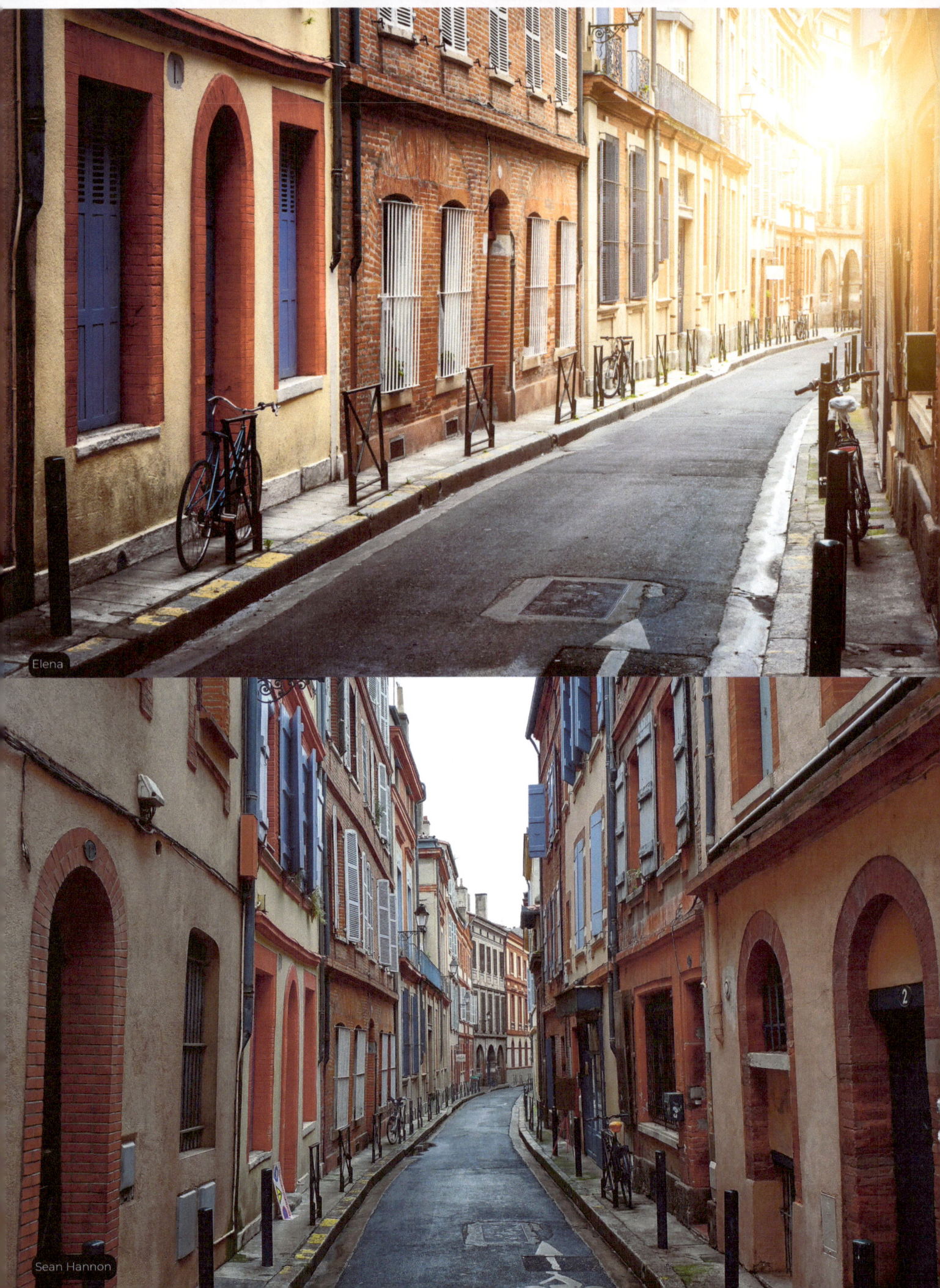

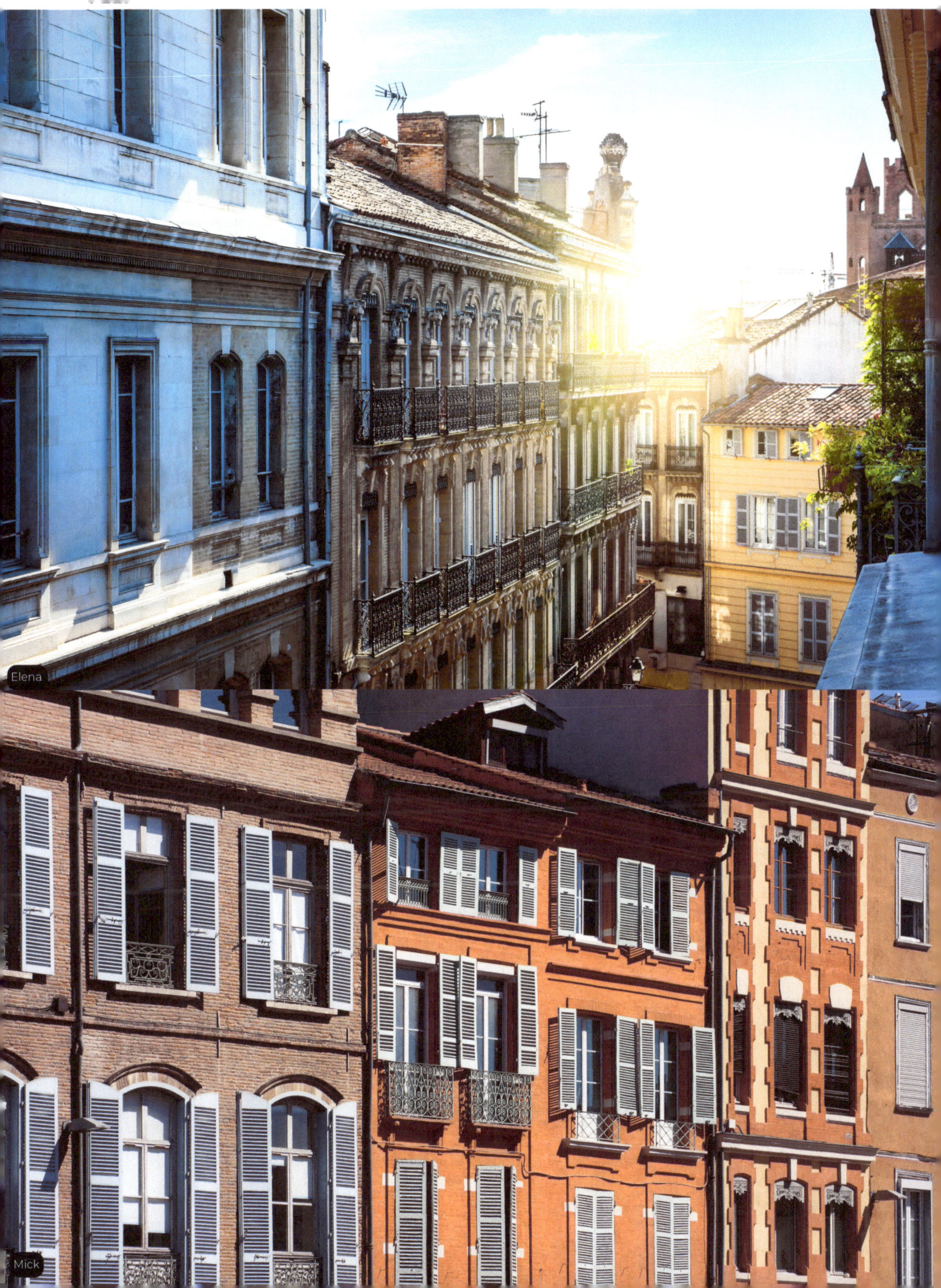

Place du Capitole

In the vibrant core of Toulouse, Place du Capitole pulsates with the rhythm of the city. This grand square, a canvas of historical and social significance, embodies the essence of La Ville Rose. Spanning an impressive 12,000 square meters, it has been the throbbing heart of Toulouse since the 12th century, resonating with centuries of civic pride and cultural evolution.

The Capitole building, a stunning edifice that dominates the square, is an architectural masterpiece. Its façade, an elegant display of neoclassical design, features eight pink marble columns, symbolizing the eight original capitouls (magistrates) of the city. The structure houses the city hall and the illustrious Théâtre du Capitole, a beacon of operatic and balletic arts.

The square itself is a lively hub, bustling with cafés, seasonal markets, and street performers. Its vast expanse is intricately laid with Occitan cross designs, paying homage to the region's rich linguistic and cultural heritage. During significant events, it transforms into a grand stage, echoing with music, celebrations, and the spirited chatter of locals and visitors alike.

Place du Capitole is not just a destination; it's an experience, an invitation to immerse oneself in the dynamic pulse of Toulouse, where history and modernity dance in harmony.

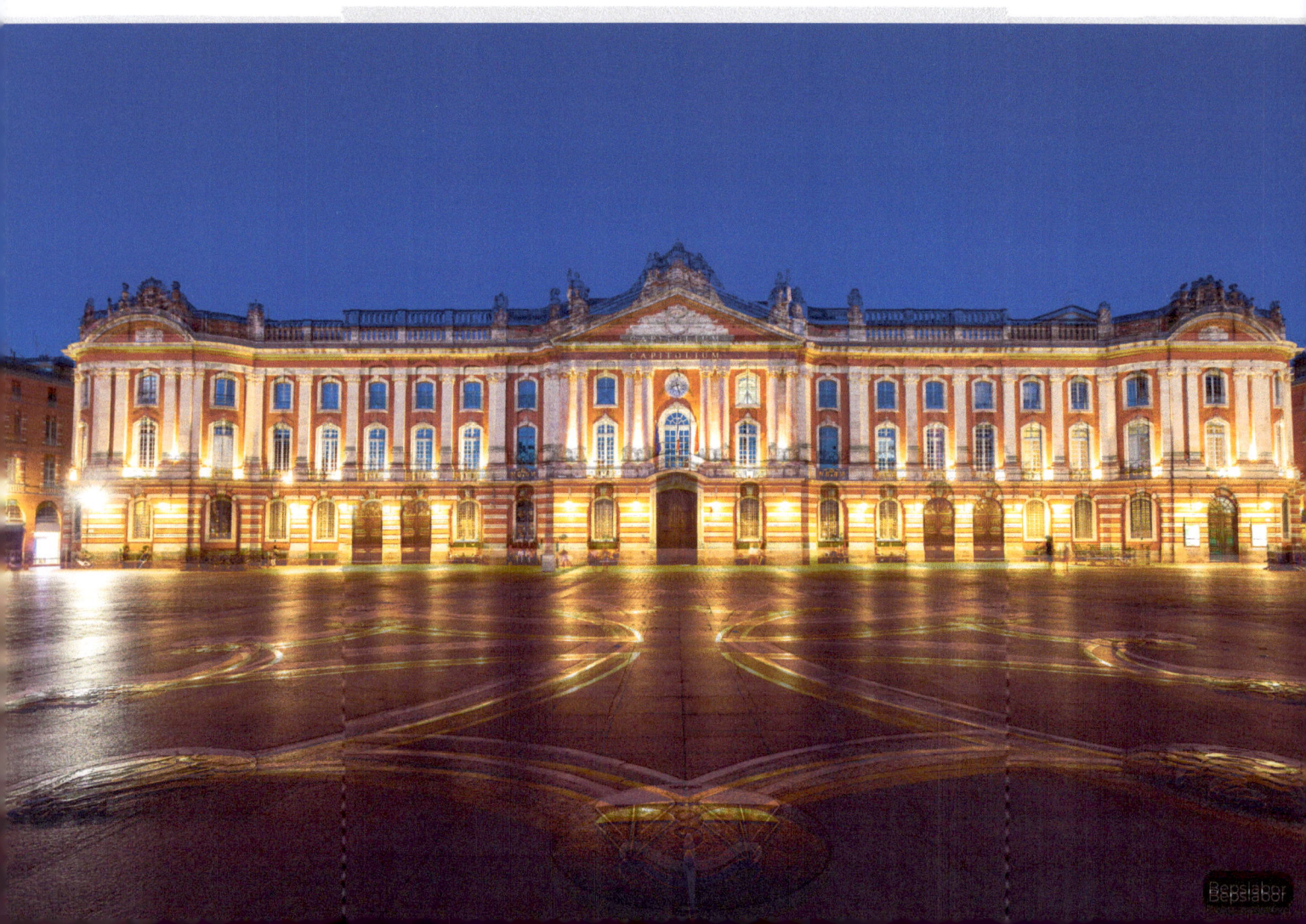

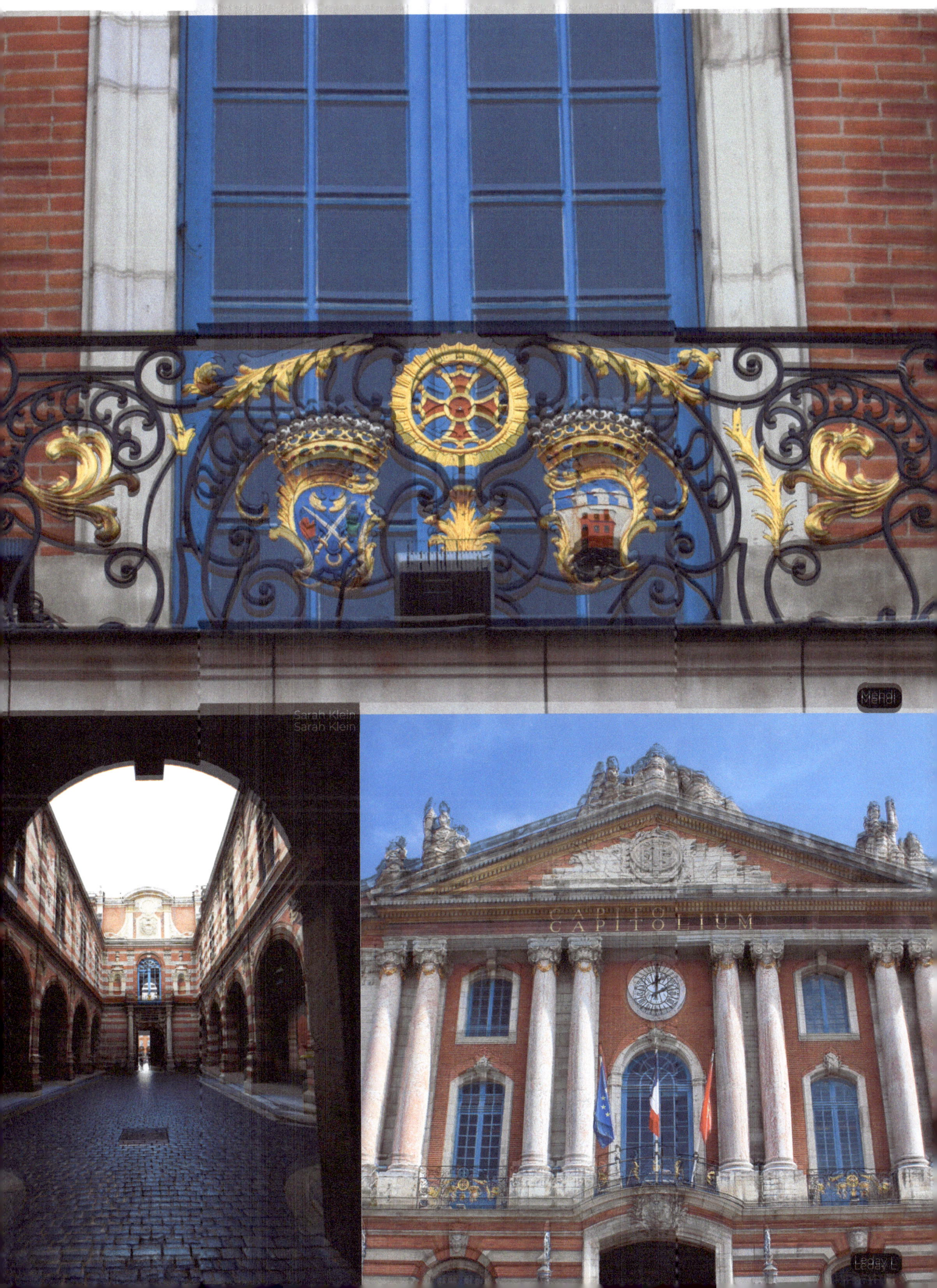

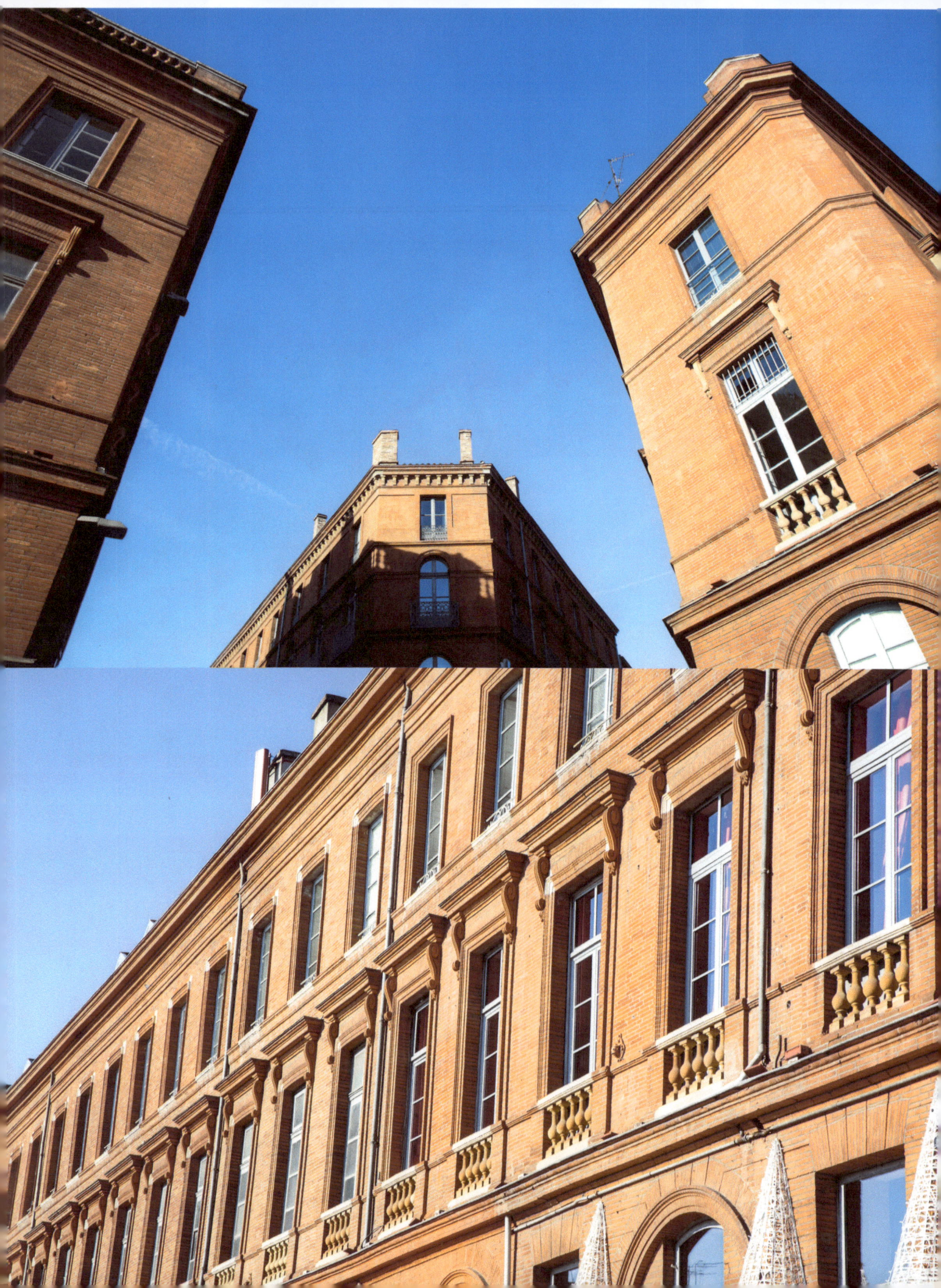

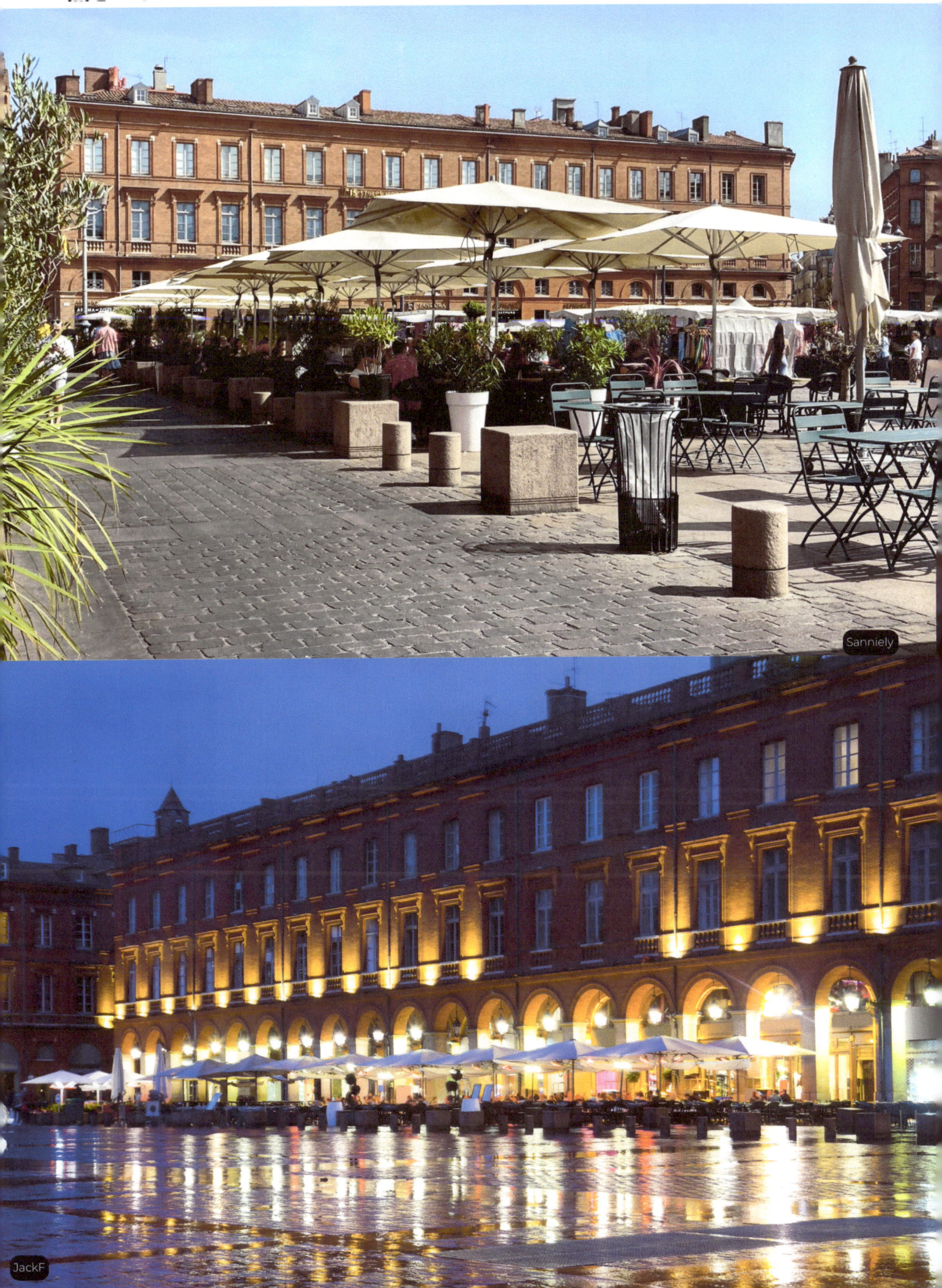

Canal du Midi

The Canal du Midi, a masterpiece of engineering and a UNESCO World Heritage site, gracefully meanders through Toulouse, offering a tranquil escape from the city's lively streets. This 17th-century canal, envisioned by Pierre-Paul Riquet, stands as a testament to human ingenuity, linking the Atlantic Ocean to the Mediterranean Sea.

Stretching over 240 kilometers, the canal's segment in Toulouse is a picturesque scene, lined with ancient plane trees whose leaves whisper tales of bygone eras. The dappled sunlight filters through their branches, casting a serene glow on the gently flowing waters. The banks of the canal are a haven for leisurely strolls, cycling, or simply basking in the idyllic setting.

Boating along the Canal du Midi offers a unique vantage point to view the city's historic architecture. From the water, one can appreciate the harmonious blend of nature and urban beauty that defines Toulouse. The canal's locks, quaint and meticulously maintained, are feats of historical engineering, still functioning as they did centuries ago.

For those seeking a moment of peace, a picnic by the canal, amidst the lush greenery and calming waters, is a delightful experience. The Canal du Midi is not just a waterway; it's a ribbon of tranquility, weaving through the vibrant tapestry of Toulouse.

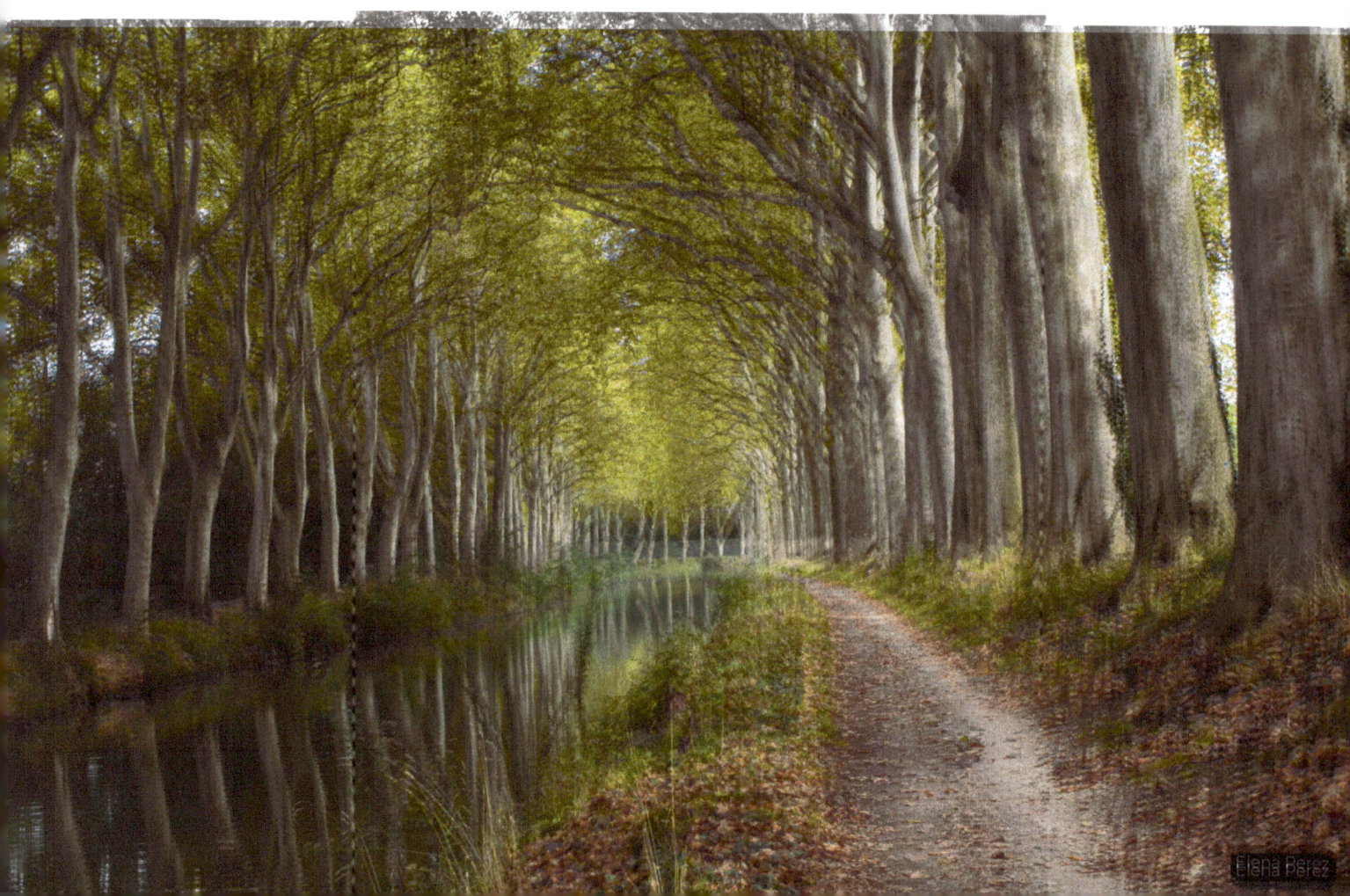

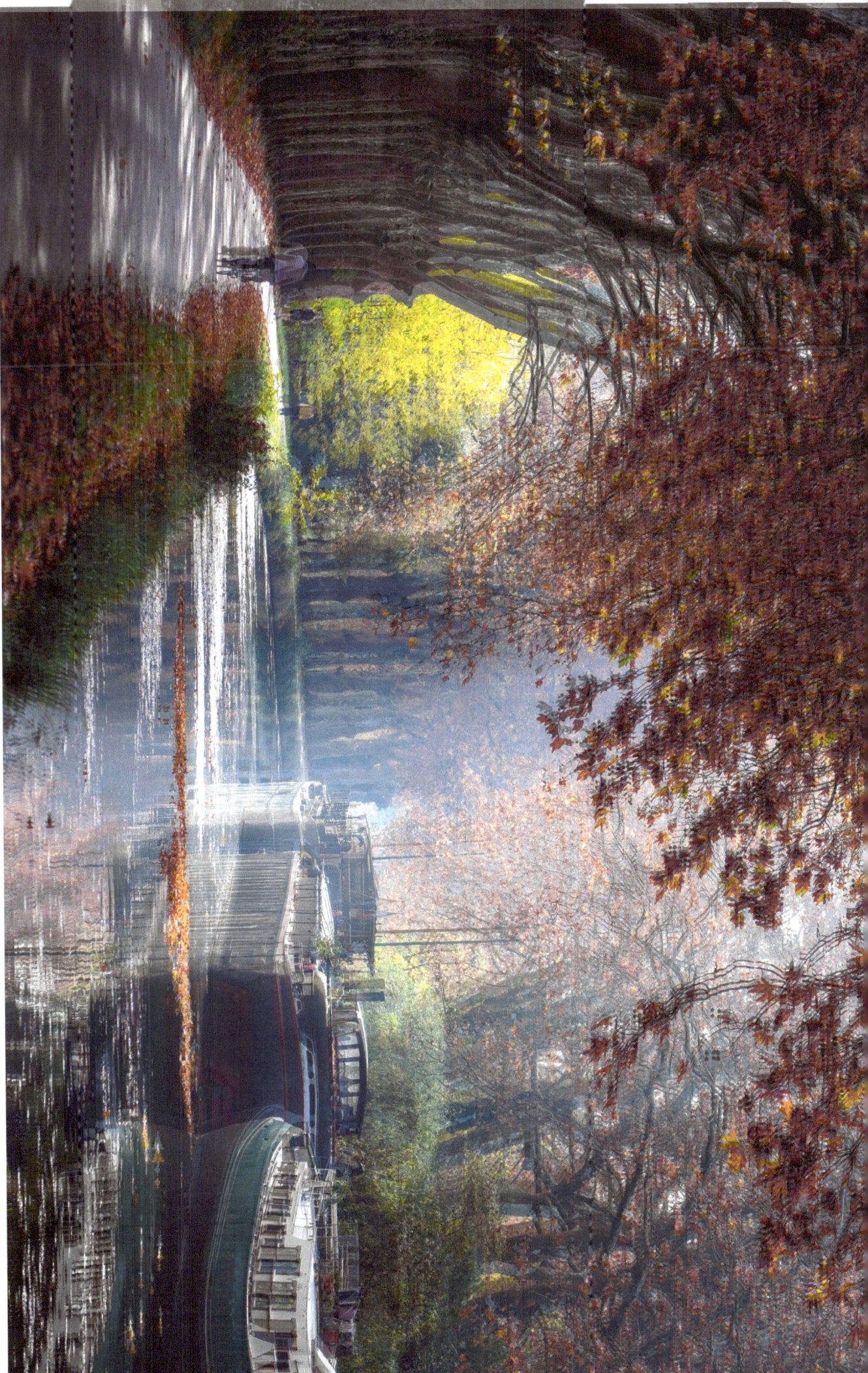

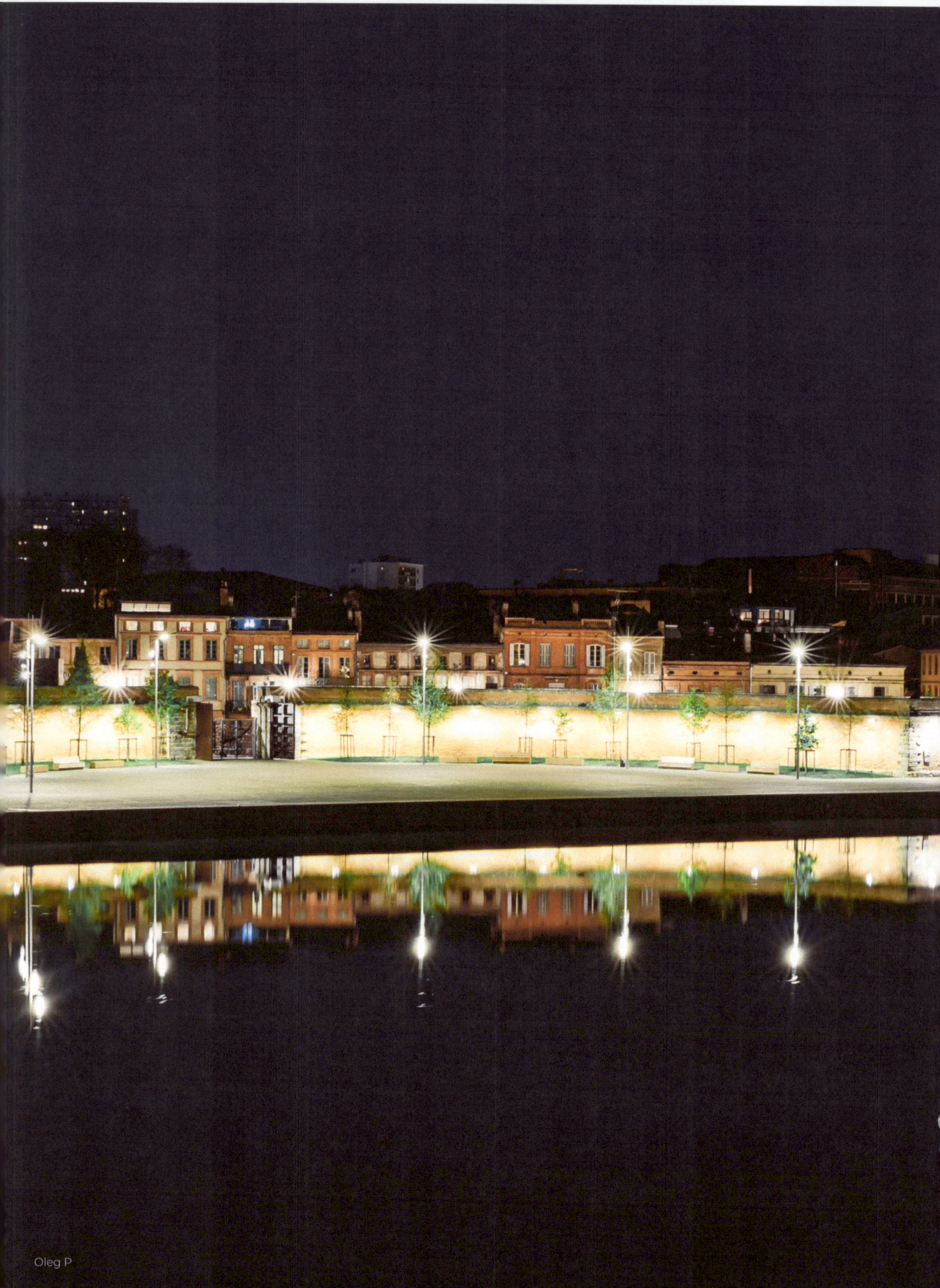

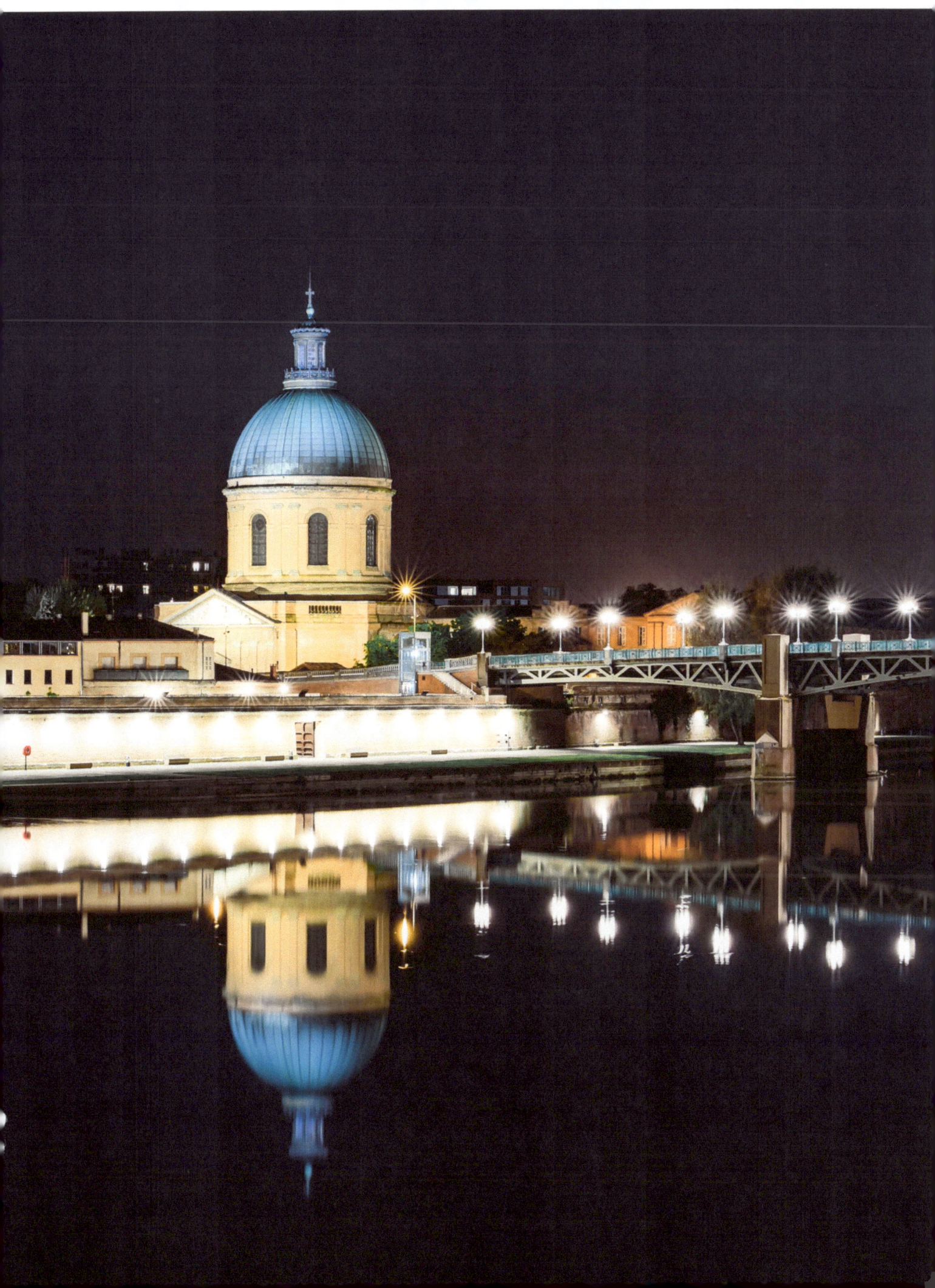

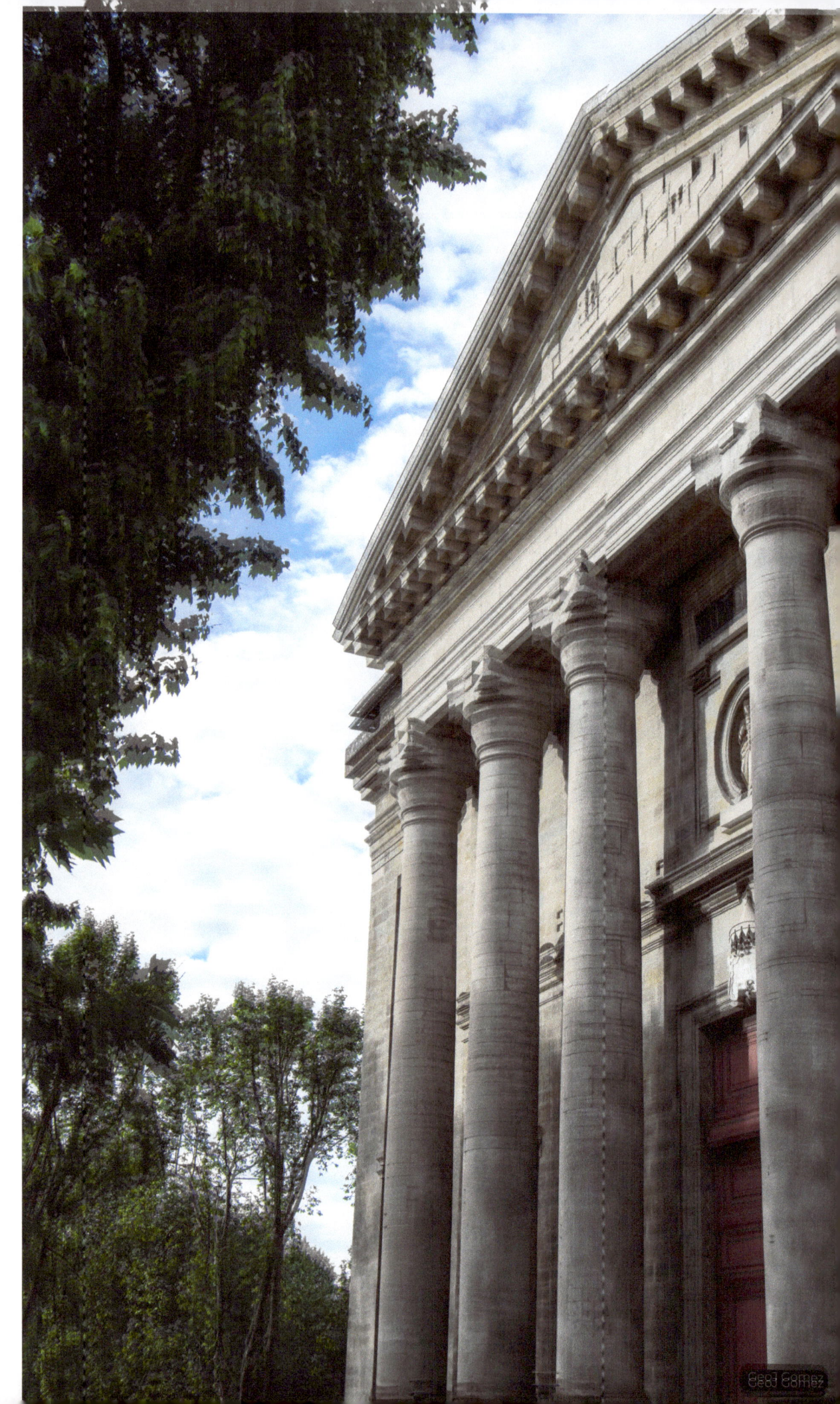

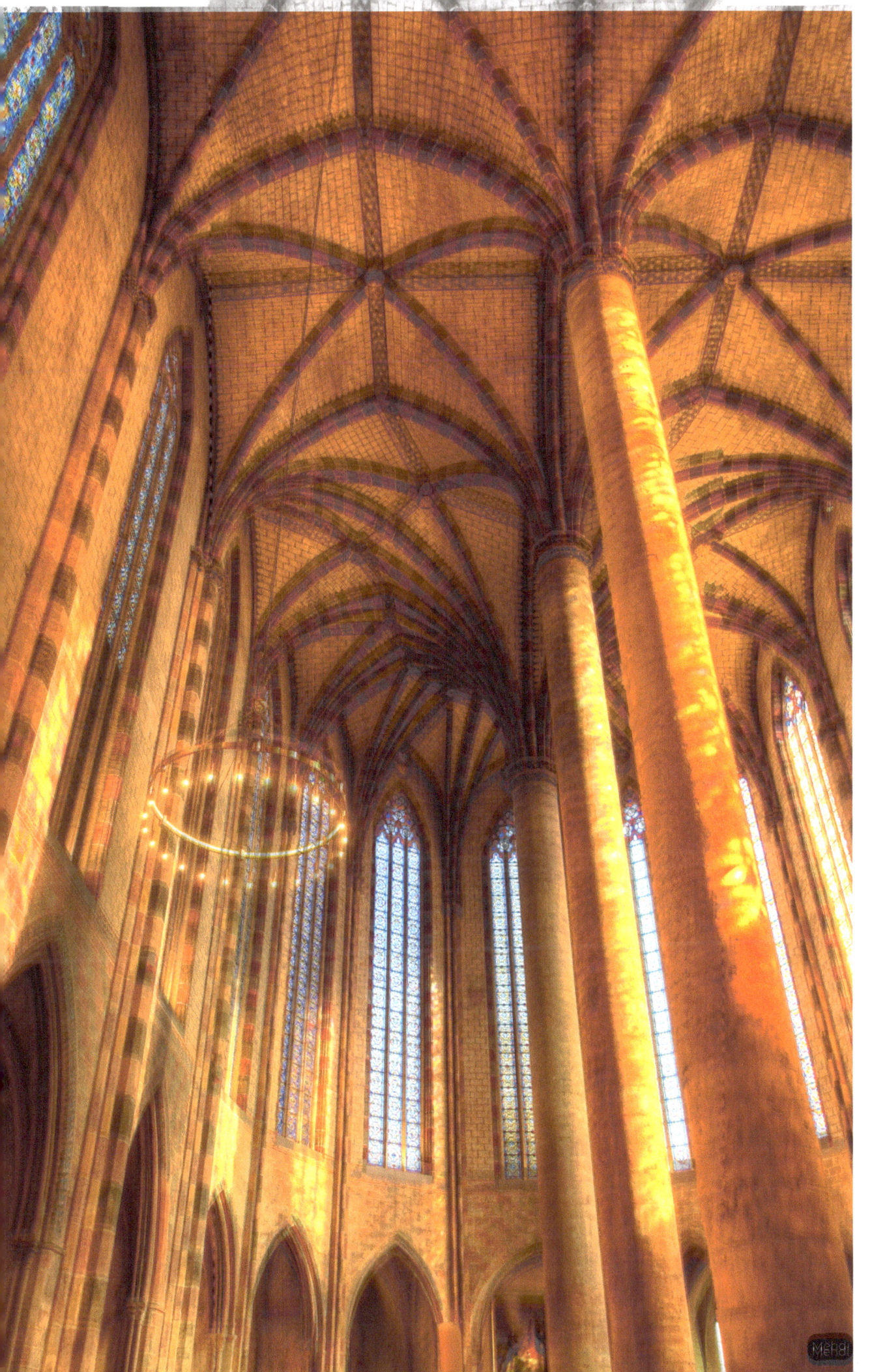

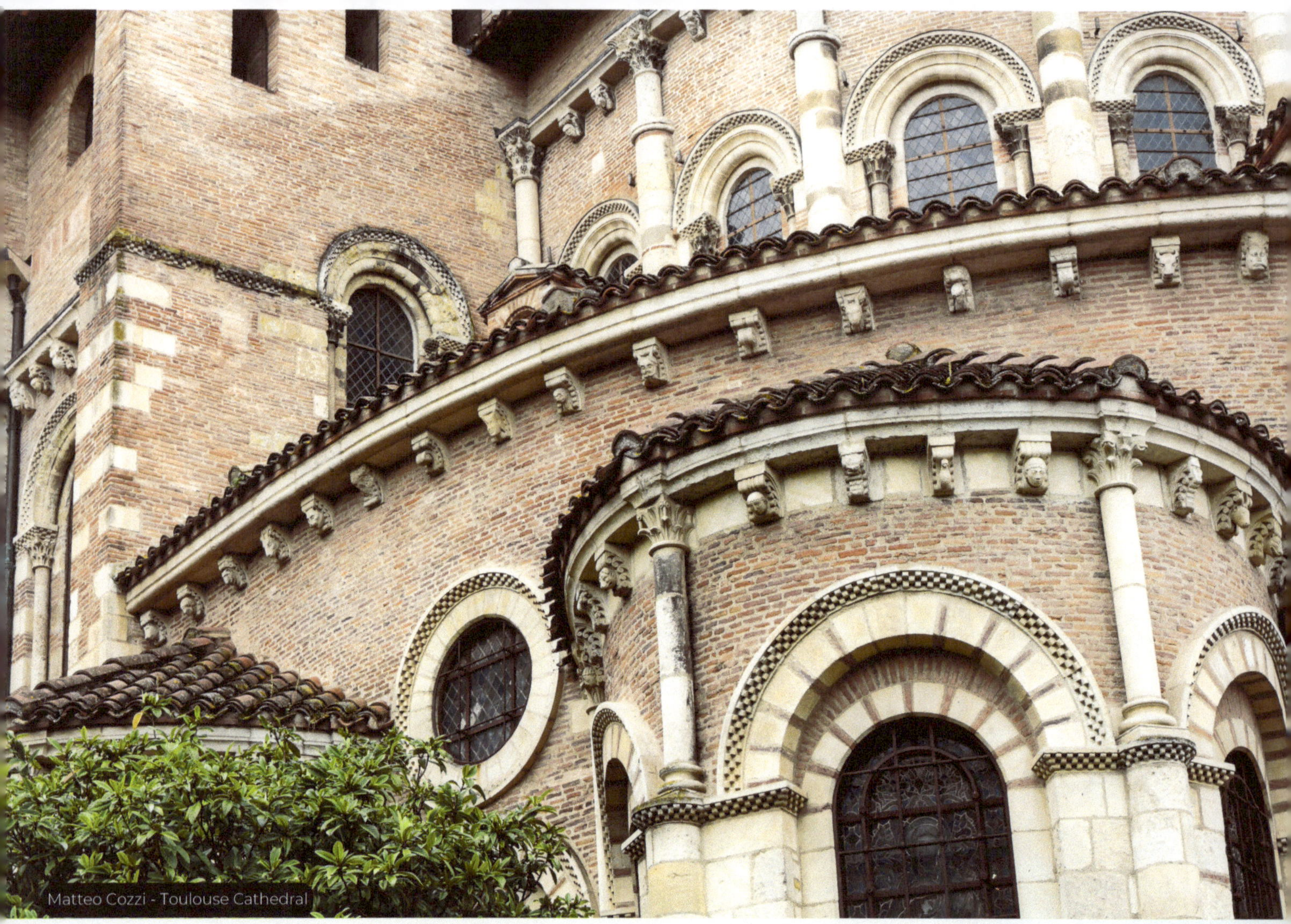

Matteo Cozzi - Toulouse Cathedral

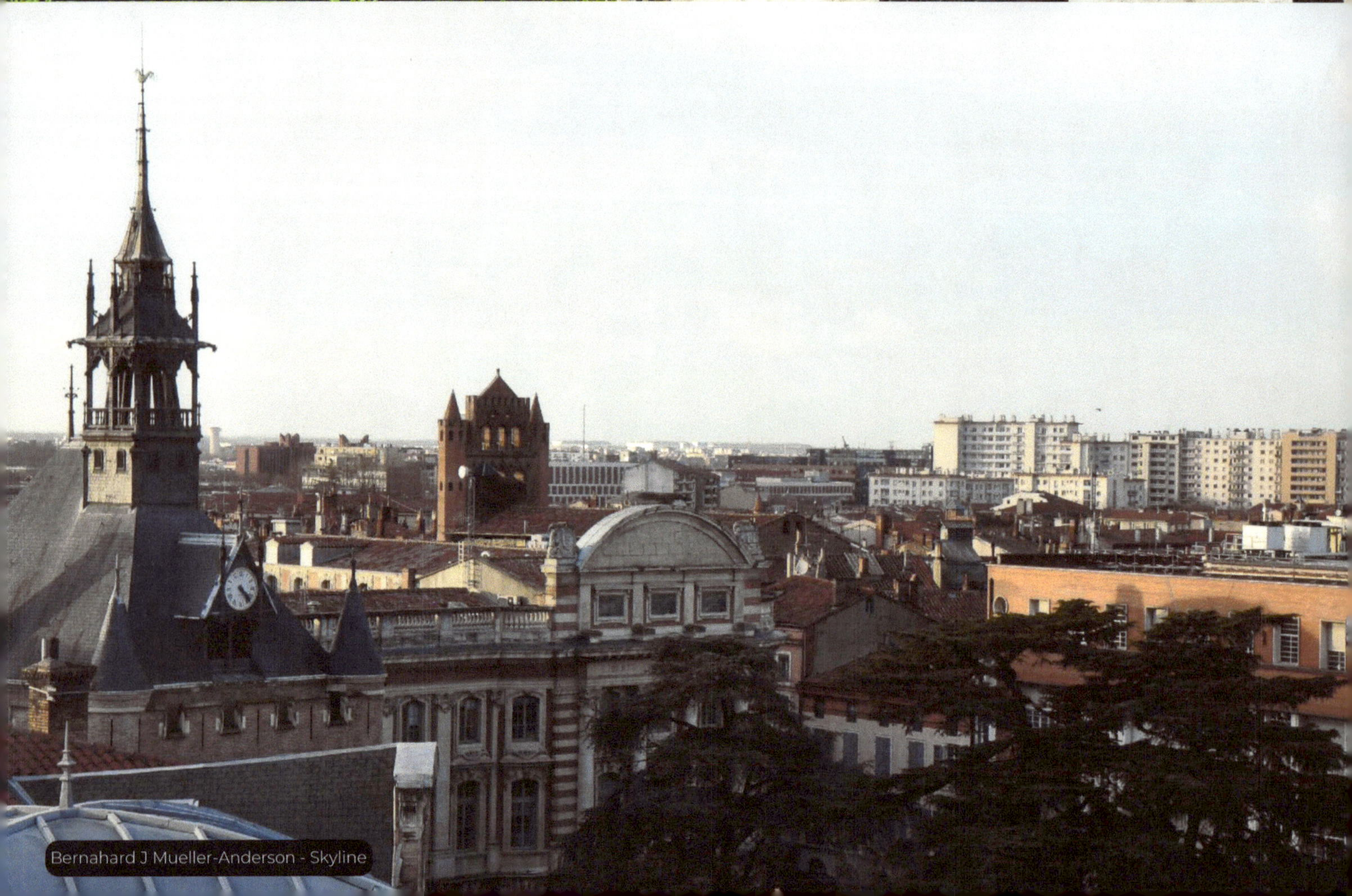

Bernahard J Mueller-Anderson - Skyline

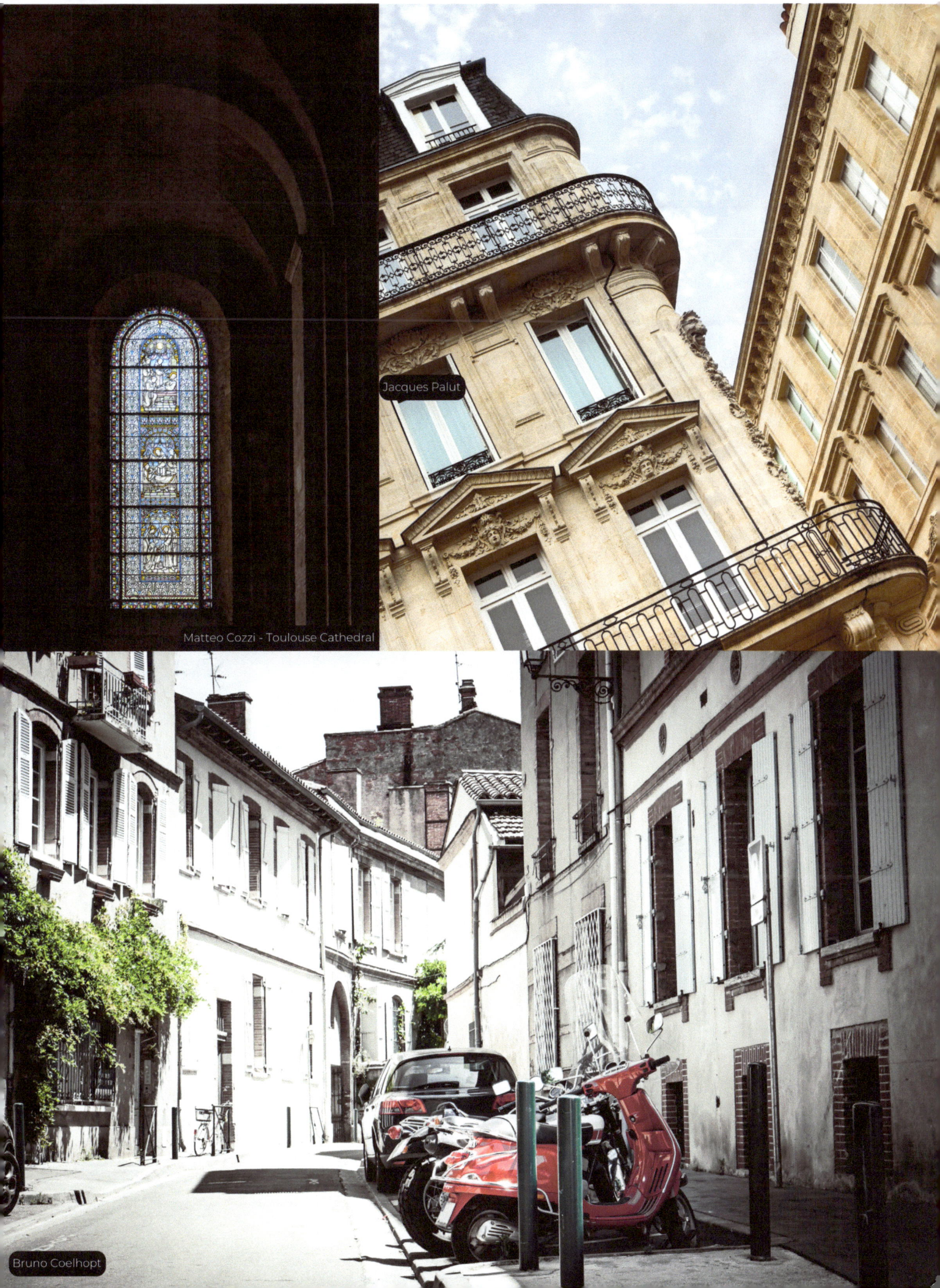

Matteo Cozzi - Toulouse Cathedral
Jacques Palut
Bruno Coelhopt

Basilique de la Daurade

Overlooking the tranquil waters of the Garonne River, the Basilique de la Daurade enshrines a spiritual and artistic heritage that resonates through the ages. Originally a Roman temple, this sacred site was transformed into a Christian basilica in the 5th century. Its current neoclassical façade, adorned with elegant columns and statues, belies a rich, multifaceted history.

The basilica's name, 'Daurade', derives from 'deaurata', Latin for 'gilded', a tribute to its once golden mosaics. Although the original structure underwent significant transformations, the essence of its ancient grandeur still permeates its walls. Inside, the atmosphere is one of solemn reverence, accentuated by the soft play of light through stained glass windows, illuminating the exquisite artworks within.

Central to the basilica's allure is the revered statue of the Black Madonna, an object of devotion since the 11th century. This venerated figure, cloaked in mystery and legend, draws pilgrims and visitors, adding to the basilica's spiritual magnetism.

The Basilique de la Daurade's location by the river adds to its charm, offering serene views and a contemplative ambience. As the sun sets, casting a golden hue over the Garonne, the basilica stands as a timeless witness to Toulouse's spiritual and cultural evolution, a serene beacon in the heart of the city.

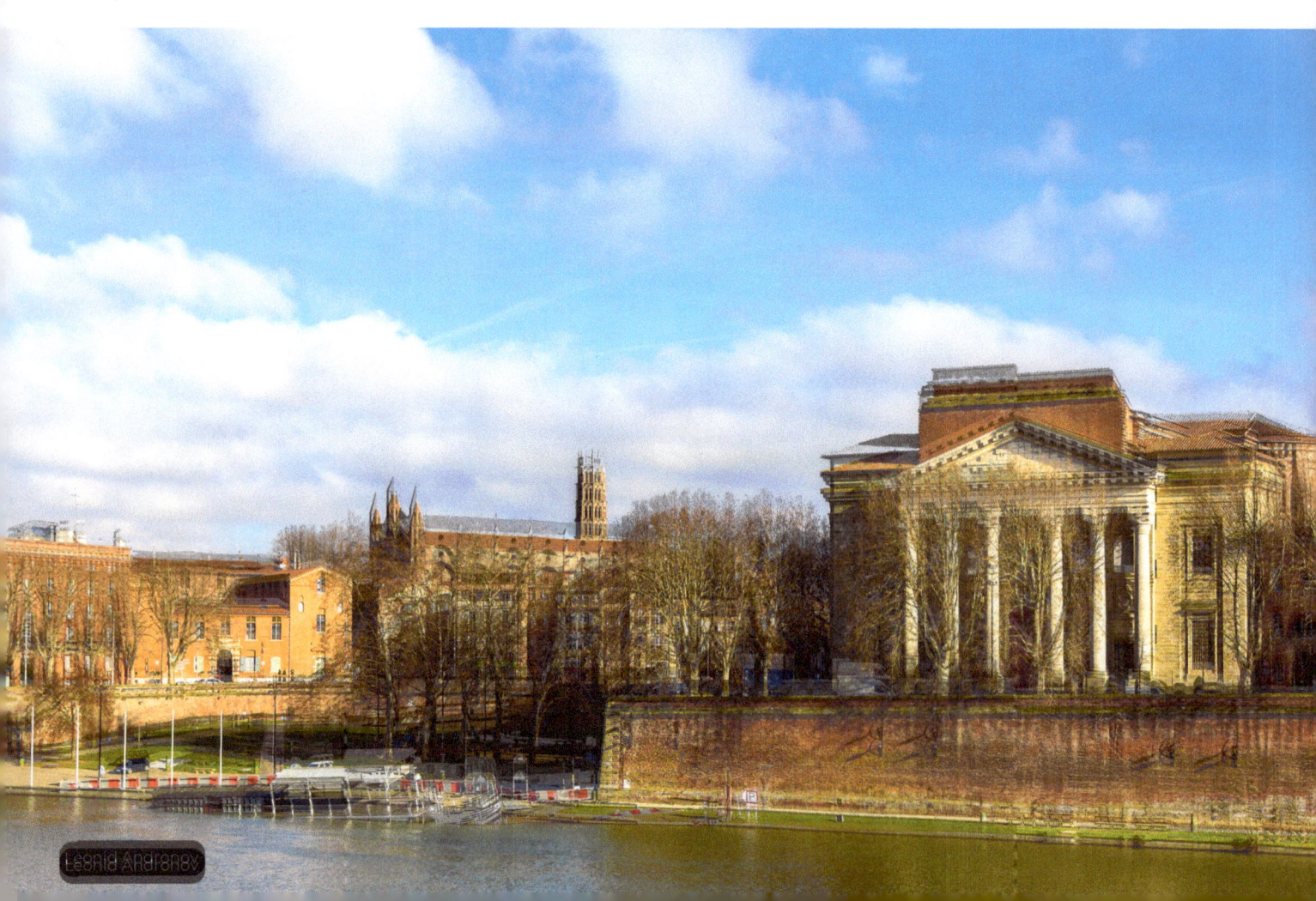

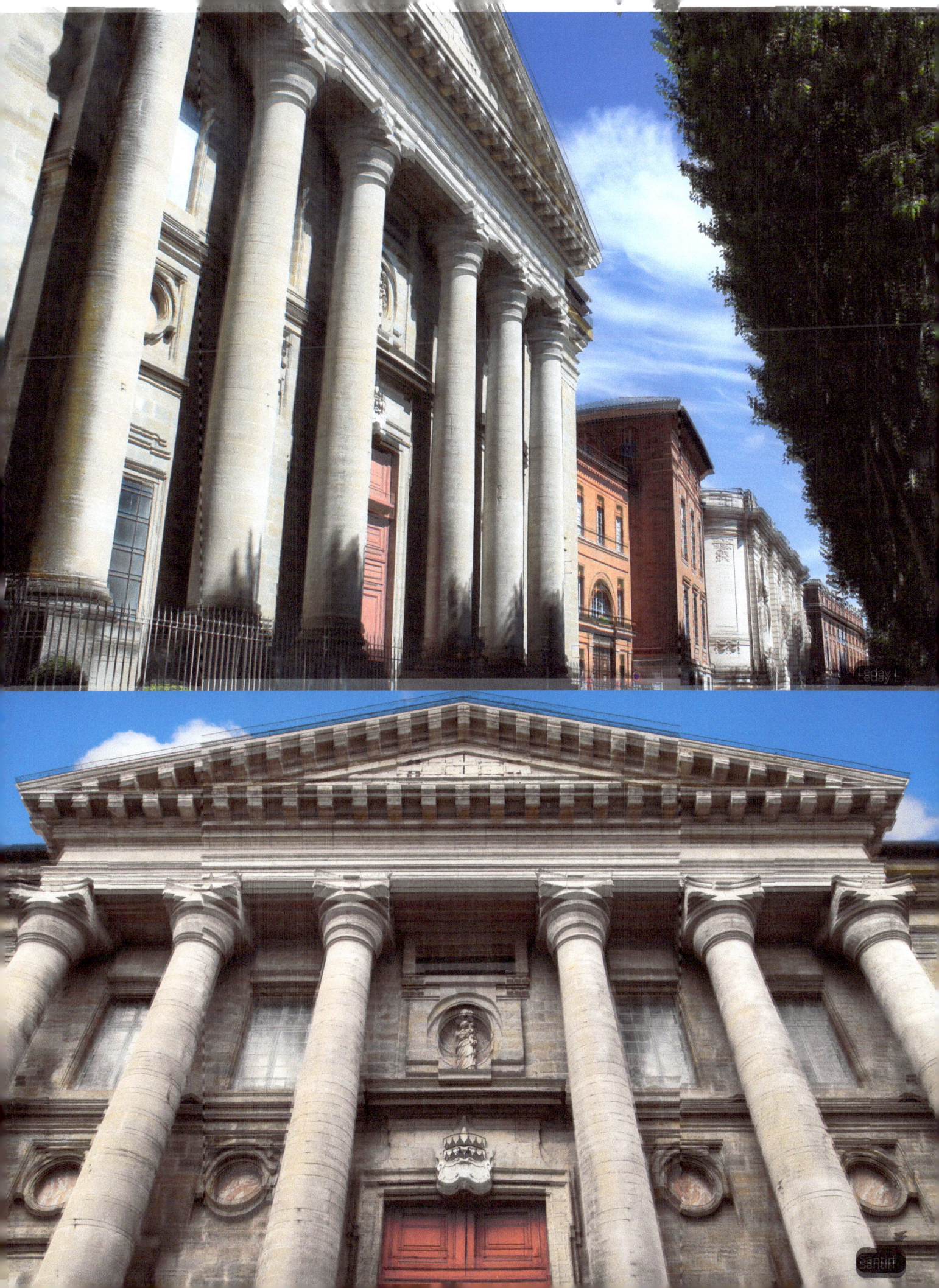

Couvent des Jacobins

In the historical tapestry of Toulouse, the Couvent des Jacobins is a woven thread of architectural magnificence and spiritual serenity. This 13th-century Gothic masterpiece, originally a Dominican convent, captivates with its majestic red brick façade, a hallmark of Toulouse's distinctive architectural palette.

Upon entering, visitors are enveloped in the convent's awe-inspiring ambience. Its vaulted ceilings soar skyward, supported by the iconic "palm tree" columns, a marvel of medieval engineering. The interplay of light and shadow through stained glass windows creates a kaleidoscope of colors, casting an ethereal glow on the ancient stone.

The convent's cloister, a haven of peace, is a harmonious blend of Gothic arches and lush greenery. Here, time seems to stand still, inviting quiet reflection amidst the bustling city. The adjoining church houses the relics of Saint Thomas Aquinas, making it a site of significant religious heritage and pilgrimage.

The Couvent des Jacobins also serves as a vibrant cultural venue, hosting concerts and exhibitions that breathe contemporary life into its historic walls. It stands not just as a monument of the past, but as a living part of Toulouse's cultural and spiritual heartbeat, bridging centuries with timeless elegance.

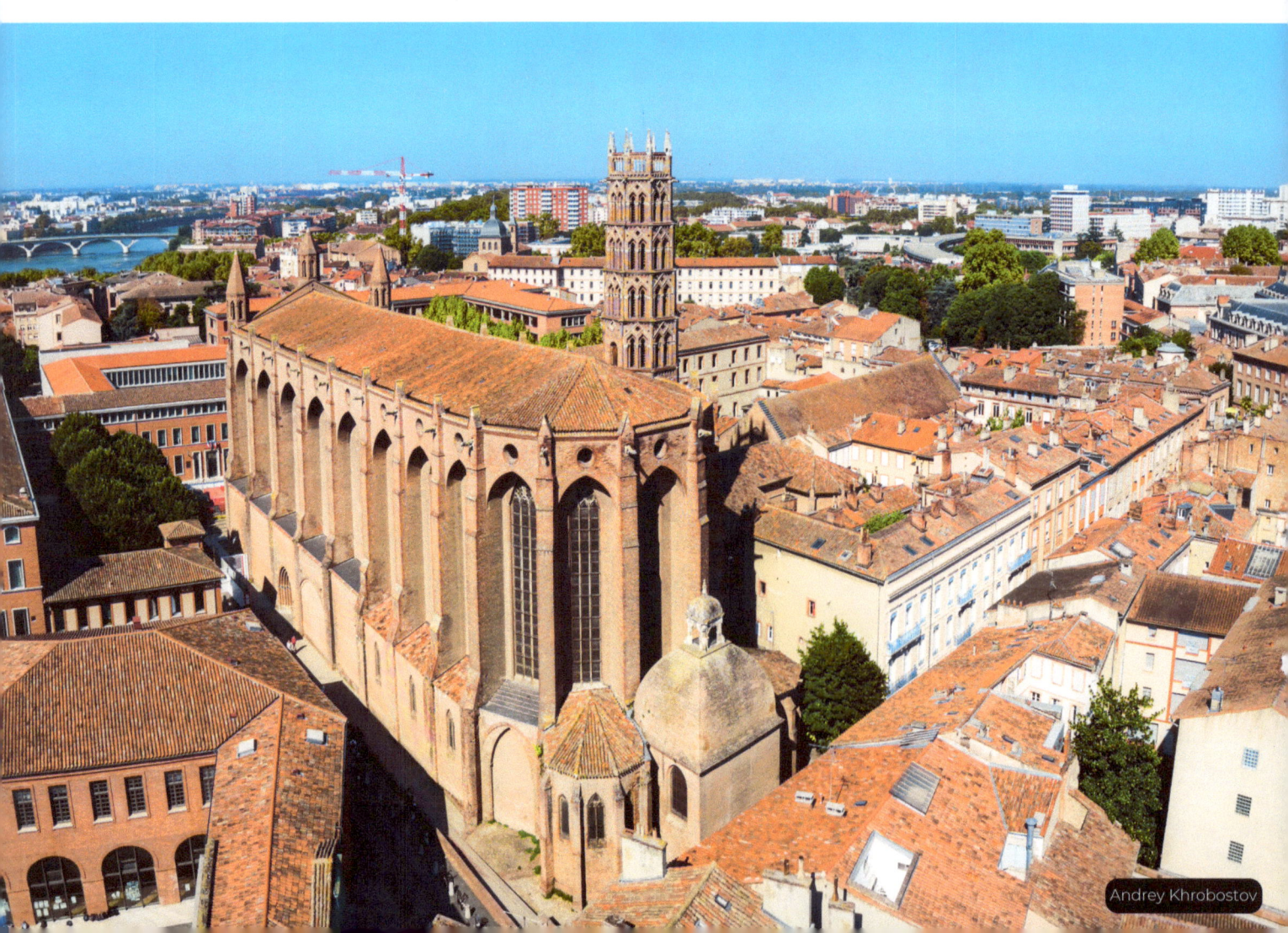

Andrey Khrobostov

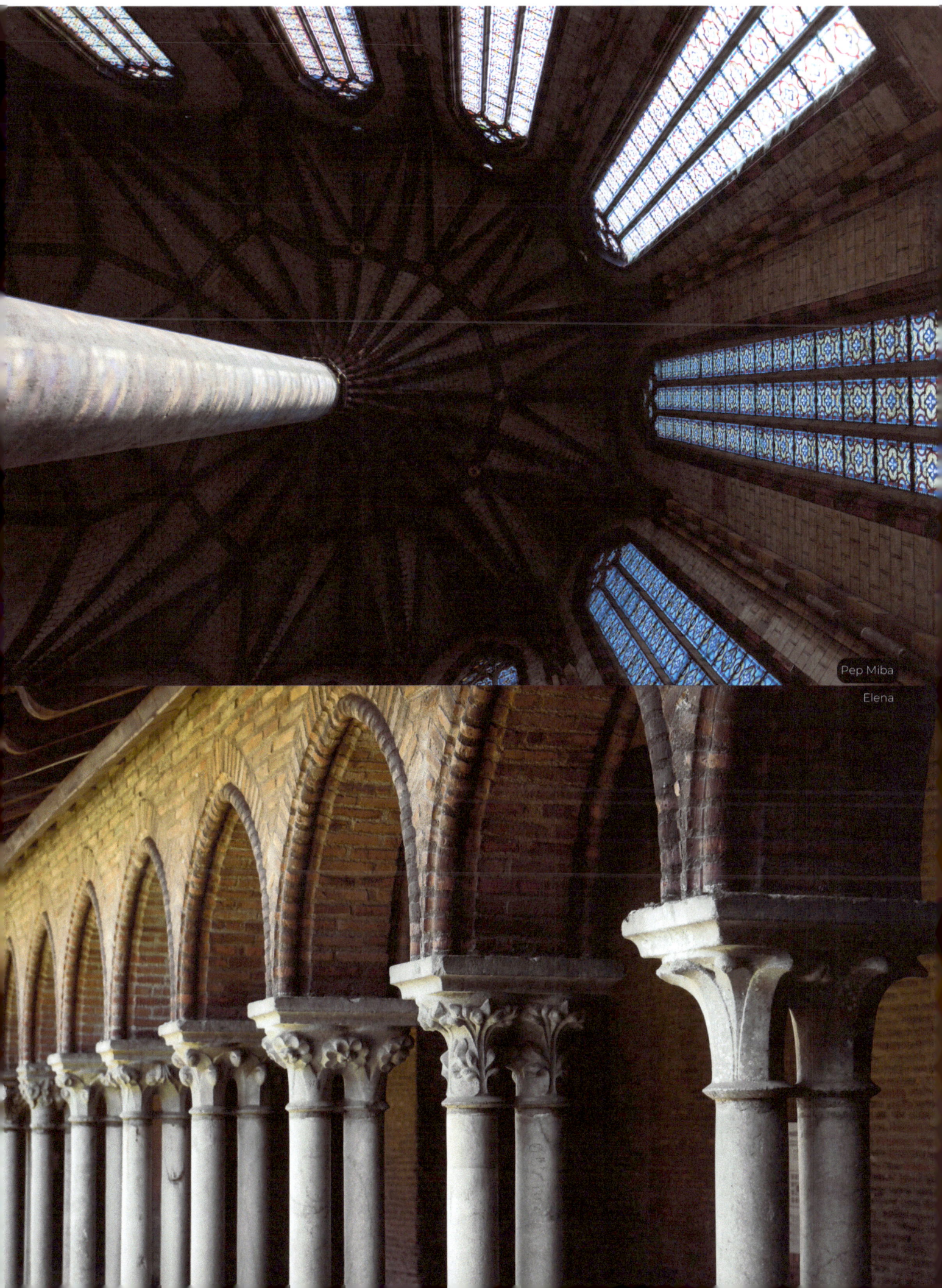
Pep Miba
Elena

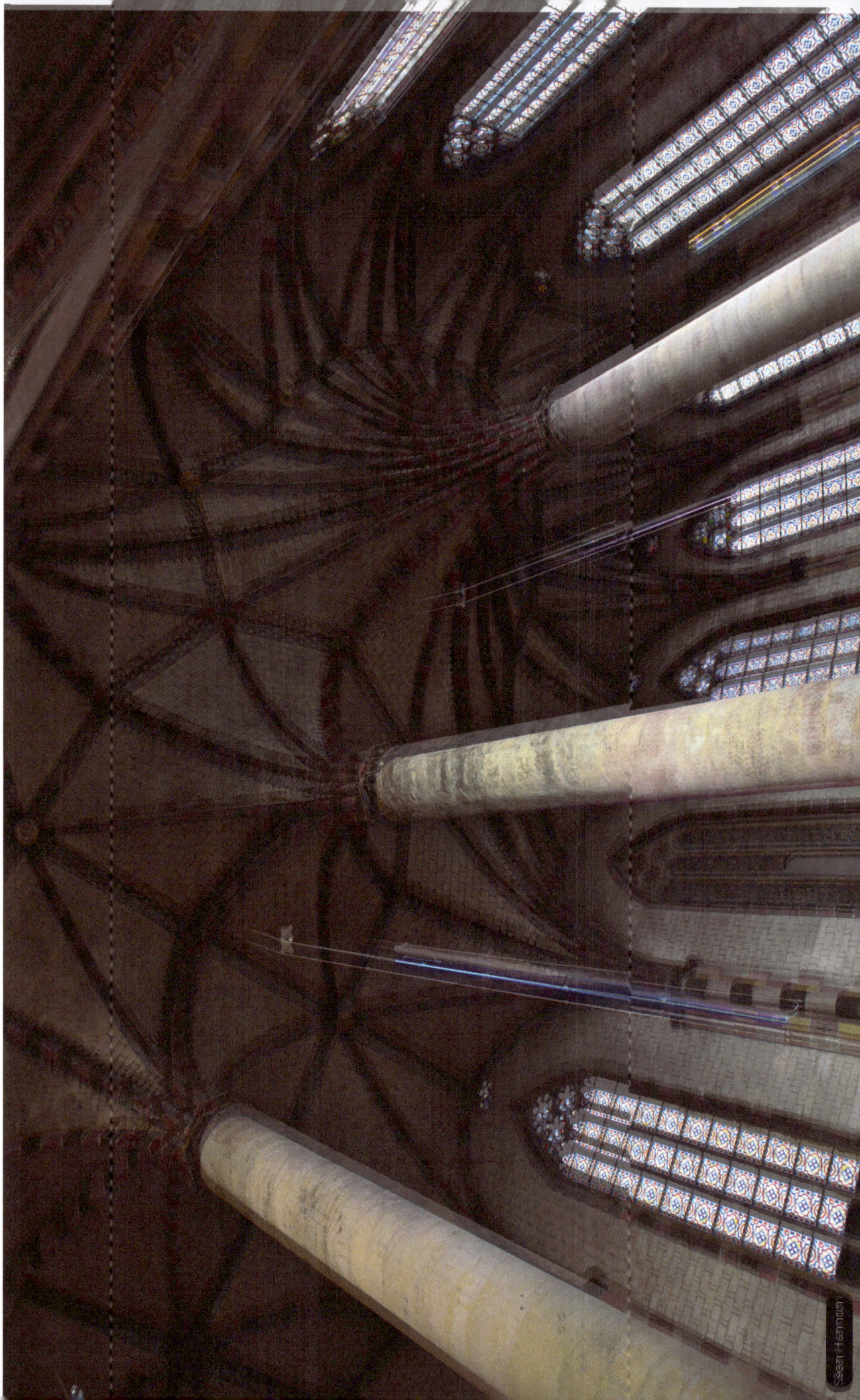

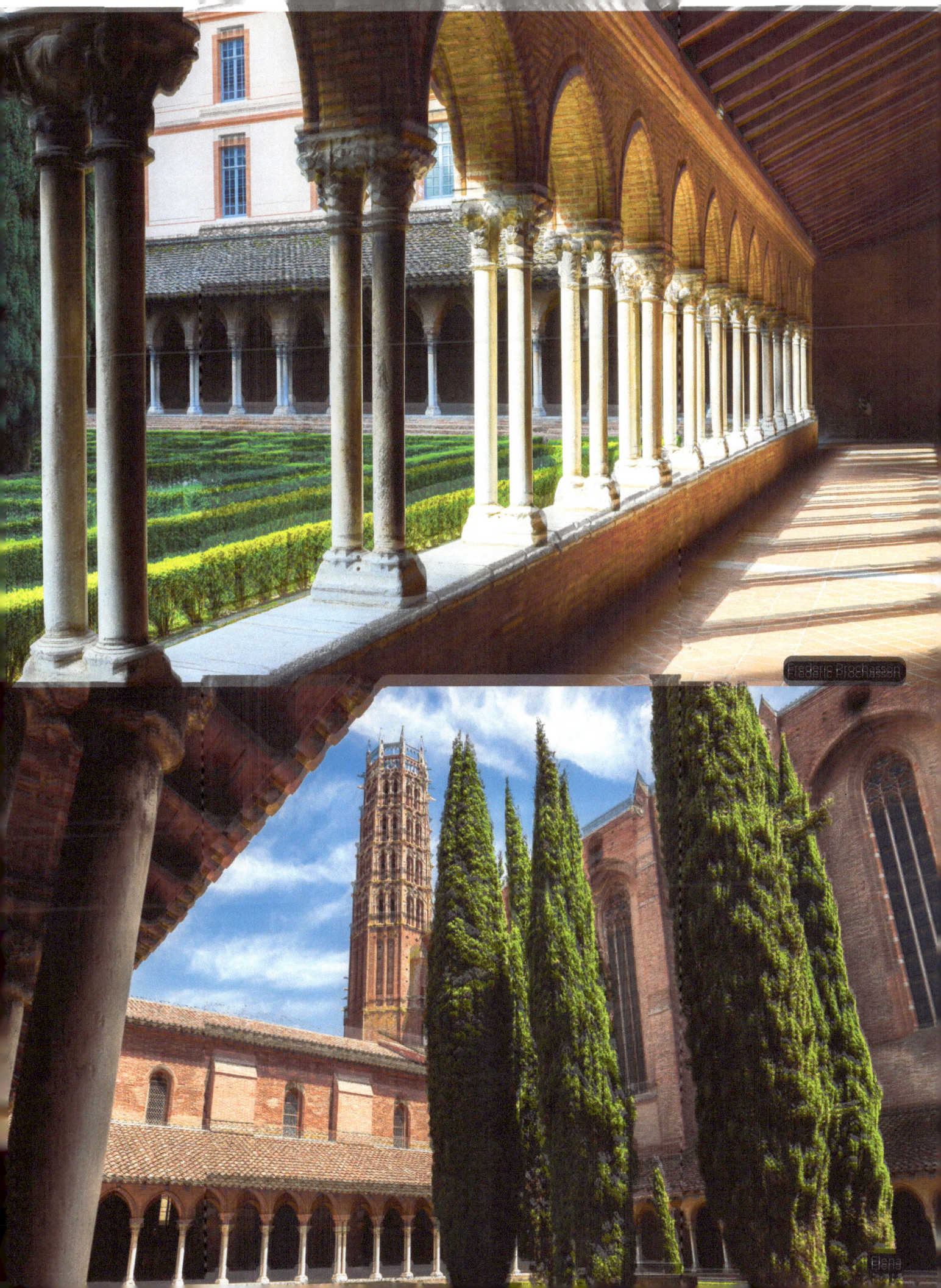

Pont Neuf

Spanning the Garonne River, the Pont Neuf is not just a bridge, but a symbol of Toulouse's enduring charm and history. Despite its name, which means 'New Bridge' in French, Pont Neuf is the oldest bridge in Toulouse, completed in the early 17th century after almost a century of construction. It has withstood the test of time, surviving floods and the changing cityscape, to become an iconic landmark.

The bridge's robust yet elegant structure, with its unique arches and circular openings designed to withstand the river's powerful currents, showcases a blend of architectural ingenuity and aesthetic grace. The pinkish hue of its stones, bathed in sunlight or illuminated by night, complements the city's famous terracotta palette.

Walking across the Pont Neuf, one experiences breathtaking views of the Garonne River, the historic riverbanks, and the city's skyline. This vantage point offers a visual narrative of Toulouse's past and present – from the serene flow of the river to the vibrant urban life along its shores.

The Pont Neuf is more than a mere crossing; it's a place where locals and visitors alike pause to admire the beauty of La Ville Rose, making it a must-visit destination in the heart of Toulouse.

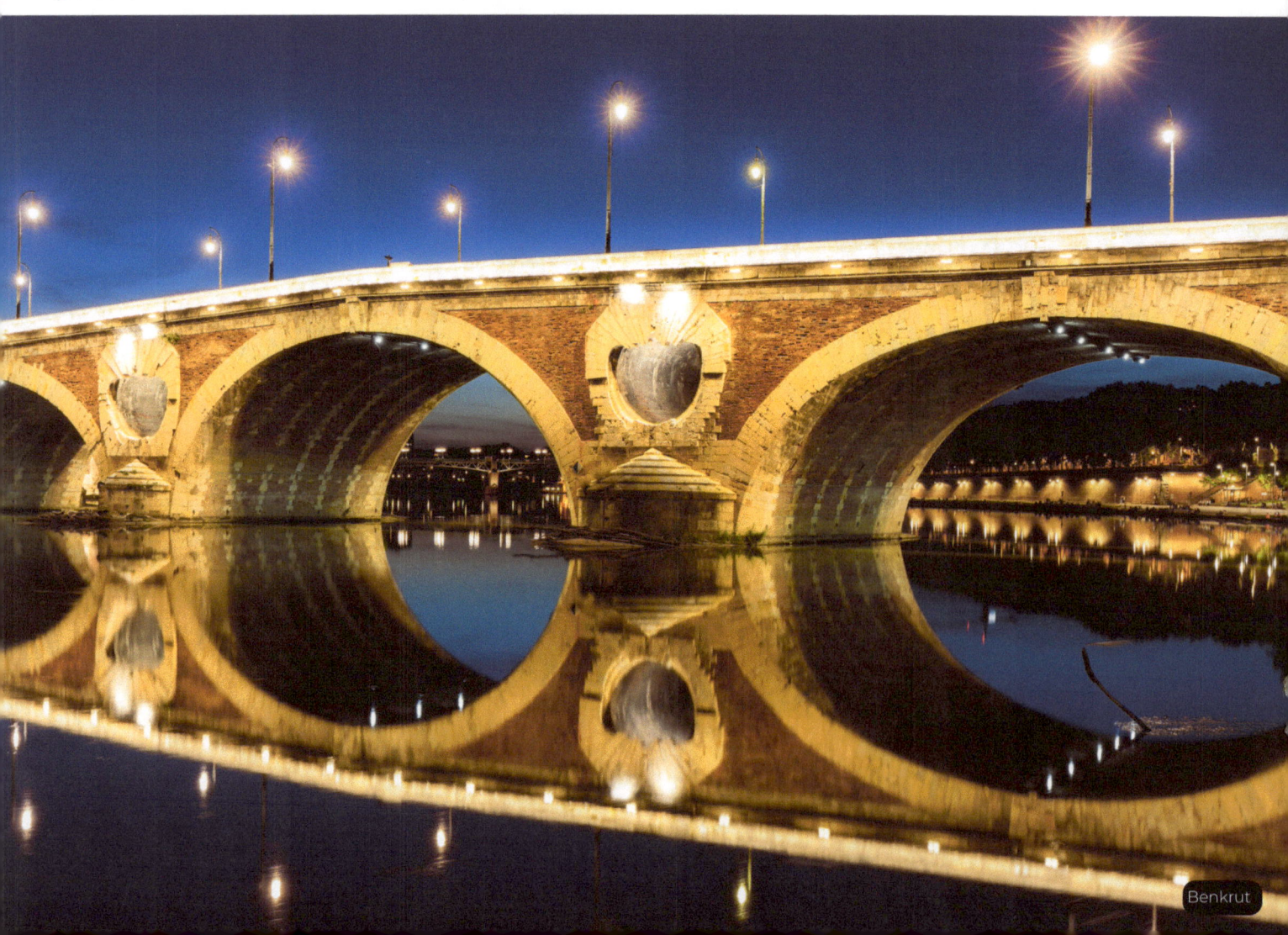

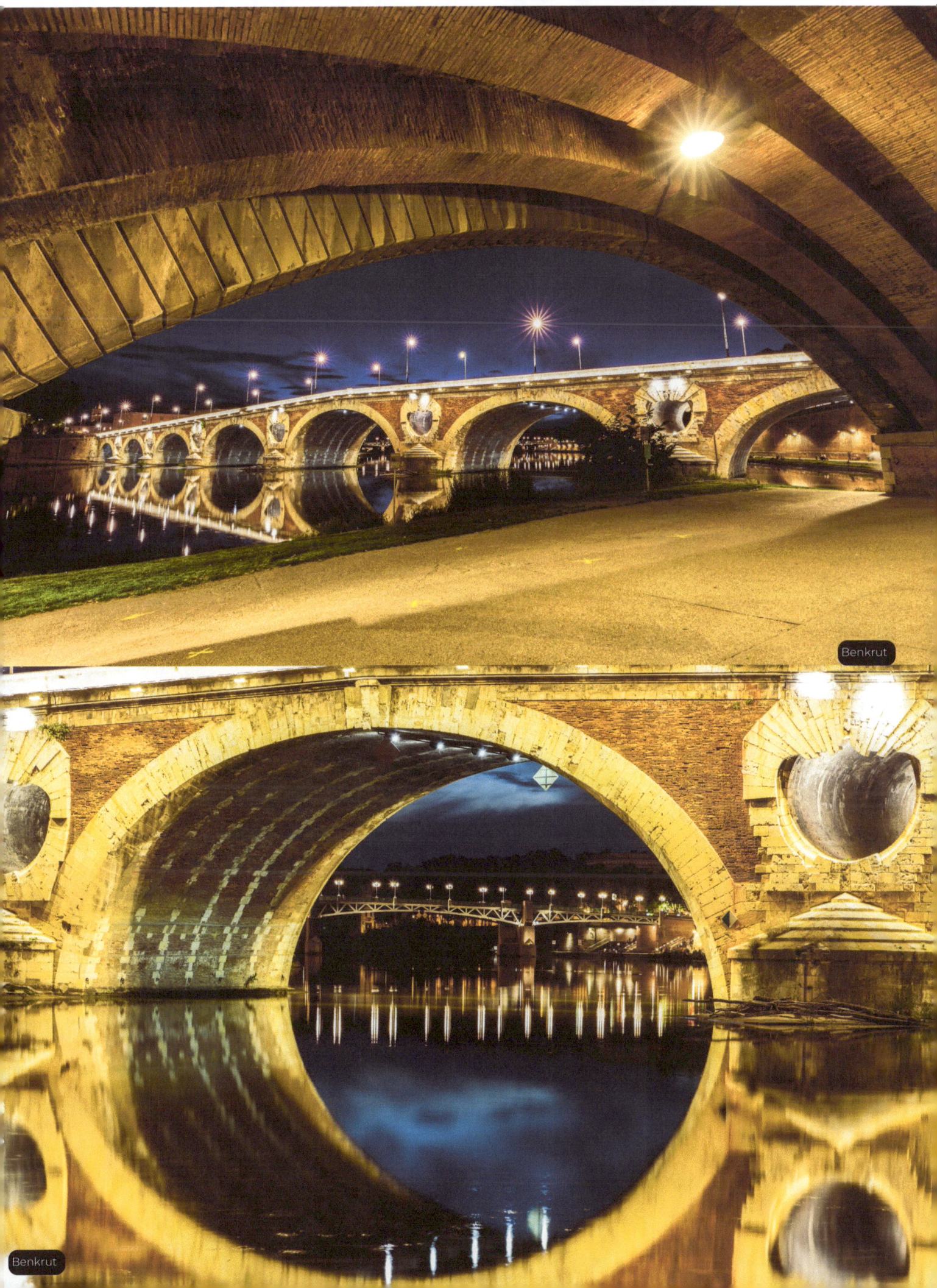

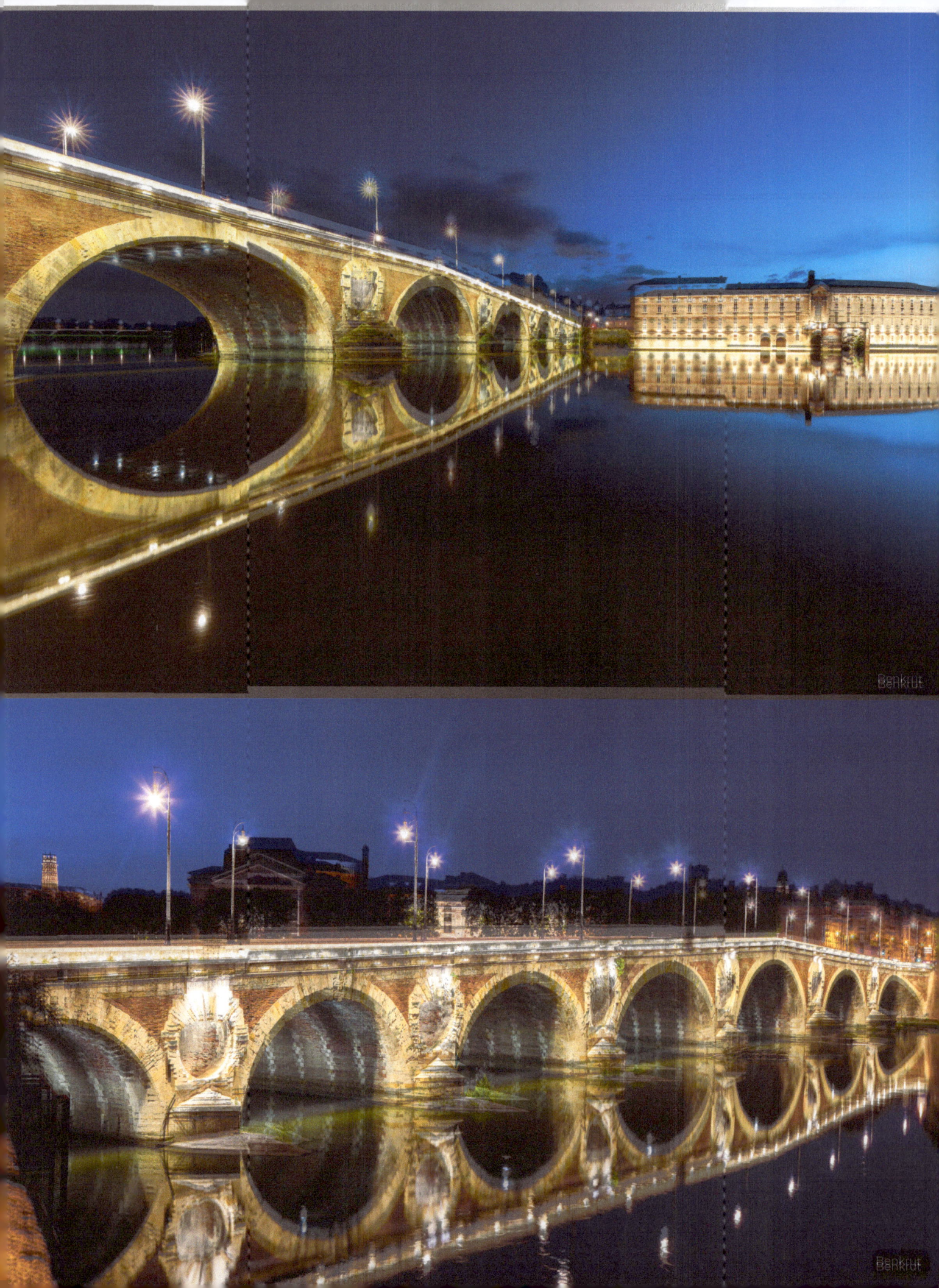

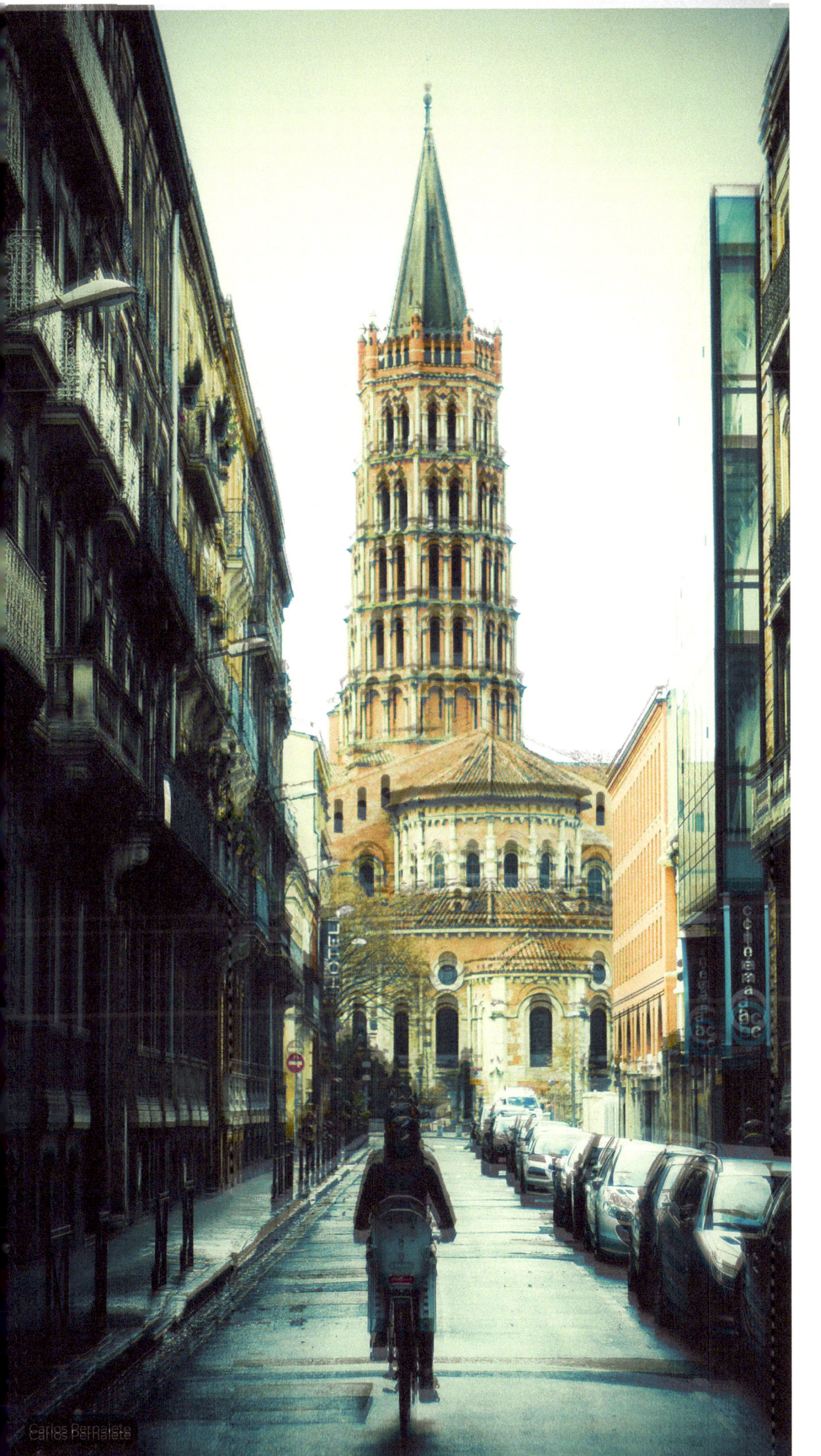

View of Basilica of St. Sernin

UNVEILING TOULOUSE

Your Travel Guide to The Pink City

As our journey through the pages of "Discovering Toulouse - The Pink City Pictorial" concludes, we hope the vivid imagery and narratives have transported you to the heart of Toulouse, illuminating its architectural splendors and vibrant spirit. For those yearning to delve deeper into the enchanting streets and hidden gems of La Ville Rose, "UNVEILING TOULOUSE - Your Travel Guide to The Pink City" awaits. This comprehensive guide is your key to uncovering new beauties and attractions, offering insightful tips and deeper explorations into the city's rich history and culture. Let "UNVEILING TOULOUSE" be your companion in discovering the endless wonders of Toulouse.

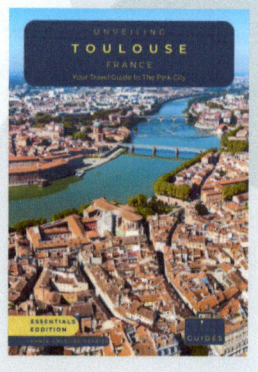

CHECK OUT THE FRANCE UNVEILED TRAVEL GUIDES SERIES

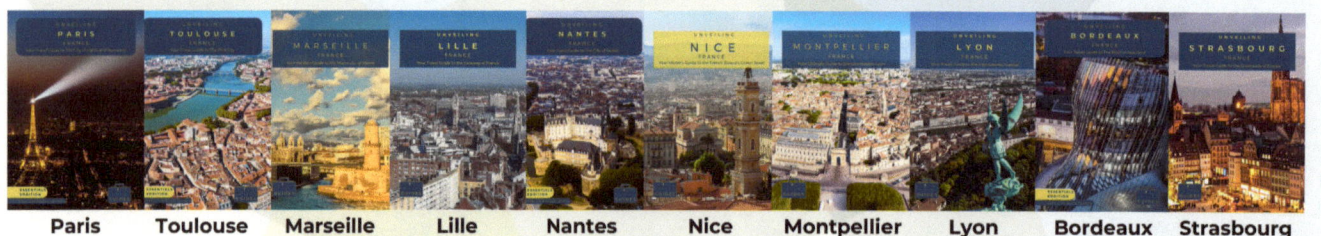

Paris | Toulouse | Marseille | Lille | Nantes | Nice | Montpellier | Lyon | Bordeaux | Strasbourg

CHECK OUT THE ITALY UNCOVERED TRAVEL GUIDES SERIES

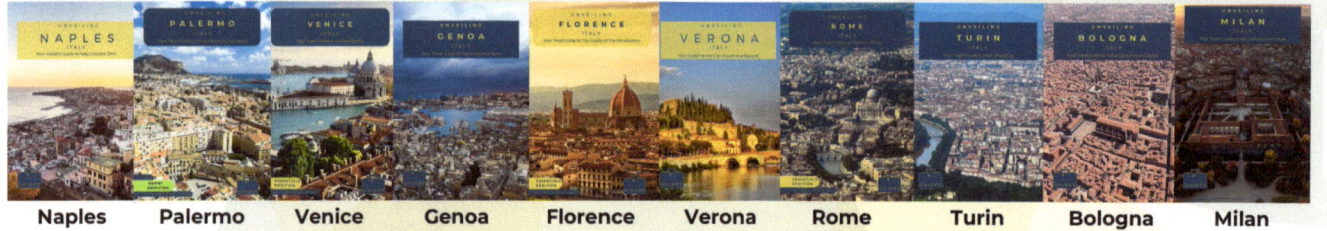

Naples | Palermo | Venice | Genoa | Florence | Verona | Rome | Turin | Bologna | Milan

CHECK OUT THE SPAIN UNVEILED TRAVEL GUIDES SERIES

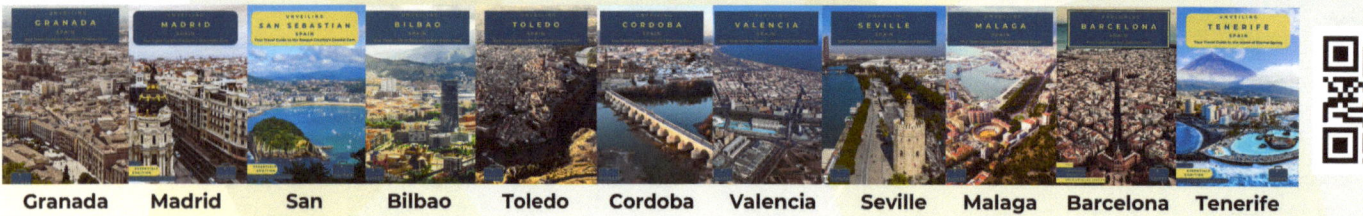

Granada | Madrid | San Sebastian | Bilbao | Toledo | Cordoba | Valencia | Seville | Malaga | Barcelona | Tenerife

Join our Tailored Travel Guides Network for more benefits by accessing this link:
https://mailchi.mp/d151cba349e8/ttgnetwork
Or by scanning the QR code

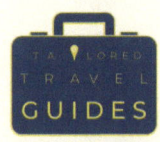

Discover your journey!

www.ingramcontent.com/pod-product-compliance
Lightning Source LLC
Chambersburg PA
CBHW051933210526
45473CB00006B/2231